ORCHIDS

ORCHIDS

Peter McKenzie Black

Hamlyn
London · New York · Sydney · Toronto

First published as *Beautiful Orchids* in 1973 by
The Hamlyn Publishing Group
London · New York · Sydney · Toronto
Hamlyn House, Feltham, Middlesex, England
Second impression 1983
Copyright © The Hamlyn Publishing Group Limited, 1973

ISBN 0 600 368874

Printed and bound by Graficromo s.a., Cordoba, Spain

Contents

An Introduction

Orchids have been grown in Europe for about 200 years, at first only by the wealthy, but for the last fifty years or so by a vast diversity of enthusiasts, a diversity applying as much to the funds available as to the characters of the growers. At every step in the progress to greater understanding of this most interesting of all families of plants enthusiasm is evident – in the selfless labours of the taxonomists down to the less selfless but no less energetic efforts of the heads of the Victorian commercial orchid establishments who poured money into expeditions sent to the jungles of the world in the hope of gain. The earlier enthusiasts had a certain similarity of background, usually academic, but today the interest is world wide and orchidists can be found in all sections of the community.

The huge family of orchids is perhaps the most interesting of all plant families if only for the staggering variation between its different members, the curious forms taken by the different genera and the widespread geographical distribution of the species; except for the Antarctic, orchids have been found in every region of the world, even in the Arctic. The particular orchids to which this book is intended to be an introduction are, however, those which grow only in the tropics and the warmer parts of the world. There is no other family of plants where so much diversity of form and colour is found. There are orchid flowers which have a pouch instead of one petal, some which have a curious tongue-like labellum or lip and yet others in which this modified petal is huge and frilled. Some species have a solitary large flower and others display a hundred all on the same stem. There is an equally wide range of colour, too; indeed, there are orchids to be found of practically every colour in the spectrum, and many types of orchid have several colours in the same bloom, the petals being different from the sepals and the lip from each. Blue is a colour seldom seen in the orchid family, however, and hybridists have spent a lifetime attempting to produce a blue orchid. Altogether orchids are completely fascinating to people of many different viewpoints – from the hybridist who

Orchids grow in a variety of altitudes ranging from sea level to high mountain elevations. This *Dendrobium sophronites* is growing at 11,000 feet on Mt Albert Edward, Papua.

A *Brassolaeliocattleya*—a hybrid between the genera *Brassavola*, *Laelia* and *Cattleya* distinguished by its enormous lip—from Hawaii

finds so many characters from which to attempt to produce new forms to the nubile lass presented with her first orchid by a hopeful admirer.

This book has been written in an attempt to discover a little of the reason for the lure of the family of orchids and with the aim of interesting beginners as well as those who have become accepted 'old hands' at orchid growing. It is now much easier to acquire a knowledge of the orchid than it was in earlier stages of the evolution of orchid lore, for a great deal has been written on all aspects of its history, starting with the recognition and listing of different species and progressing to their classification and latterly to their management. Many of these earlier works make absorbing reading but they are probably most enjoyable to those who deal either with plant physiology or the practical cultivation of orchids.

The first known references to orchids are found in eastern literature in the writings of Confucius, a Chinese sage born in 551 B.C., who notes particularly their fragrance. The Chinese word for orchid is *ran* or *lan,* a typical quotation from Confucius being 'Ran gives the king's fragrance', and this word recurs in the works of other poets and philosophers as the epitome of purity, grace and fragrance. The first references to particular species occur in Chinese and Japanese literature contemporary with the early Christian era. For example, the Chinese Minister of State Ki Han, in a work written in about A.D. 300, mentions two orchids now known as *Cymbidium ensifolium* and *Dendrobium moniliforme,* descriptions of which frequently crop up in writings of this period.

Several other books were written in Chinese from this time up to the middle of the eighteenth century and many paintings and drawings made, some of which still exist. Most of the orchids described were cultivated and admired for their aesthetic value, the delicacy and refinement of their flowers, and were almost invariably fragrant, for according to the old proverb 'A flower without fragrance is like a woman without virtue'. What is probably the very first book on orchid cultivation was written in Chinese in about A.D. 1,000 and lists not only species and varieties, but gives cultural instructions.

At the beginning of the eighteenth century the Emperor of Japan commanded Joan Matsuoka to write a book on orchids which was, however, not published until 1772, after the author's death. The book was rewritten in Chinese and describes and illustrates species and many of their varieties. It gives detailed cultural instructions covering the day to day management of the plants, even including the treatment for the control of insect pests.

It is clear that the cultivation of orchids in China and Japan was an occupation of the aristocracy, who not only raised exquisite forms of species but, especially in China, commissioned artists and writers to make paintings and produce books about them. Even the Shogun, the hereditary commander-in-chief of the army and virtual ruler of Japan until 1867, had his favourite orchid plants which he carefully cultivated himself.

In the west, however, the interest in orchids was mainly medicinal. They are first mentioned in *The History of Plants* and *The Causes of Plants* of Theophrastus, a pupil and friend of Aristotle who was born on the island of Lesbos in about 370 B.C.

The title-page of Gerard's *Herball*, 1636. By the time this enlarged edition was published fifty orchids were known—for their medical use—in the west.

He first gave them the name orchis, the Greek word for testicles, from the shape of the paired underground bulbs of the species found growing round the Mediterranean. Dioscorides, writing in about A.D. 100, described two orchids among the 600 other plants in his *Materia Medica* and, furthermore, specified their function in medicine. According to the Doctrine of Signatures formulated by the Greek herbalists, the medicinal use of a plant was determined by its form or appearance. The orchis was consequently believed to be useful in promoting fertility and virility. This belief lasted in Europe until well into the eighteenth century owing to the almost religious reverence in which the ancient Greek philosophers were held.

9

These orchids illustrate some of the variety of colour, shape and habit of growth found in the Orchidaceae: a Caribbean *Vanda* with a triangular lip (top left); *Dendrobium primulinum*, an epiphytic species from Nepal (bottom left); *Calypso bulbosa*, one of the many terrestrial orchids found in the north temperate zone, even as far north as Alaska (above); *Orchis palionacea*, the temperate zone 'Butterfly Orchid' (top right); and *Paphiopedilum haynaldianum*, a terrestrial species from the Philippines.

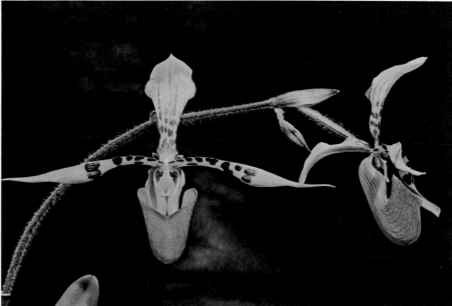

The middle of the fifteenth century saw the invention of printing and also the beginning of a long line of books and writing connected with orchids. At first this was no more than the inclusion of orchid species in plant lists and herbals for their supposed medicinal qualities. For example, Otto Brunfels of Strasburg lists six orchids among the 240 plants contained in his *Contrafayt Kreuterbuch* published in 1537, while in another herbal which appeared at about the same time, the *Historia Stirpium* of Leonard Fuchs (after whom the Fuchsia was called), eleven orchids are named. By the time the enlarged edition of John Gerard's famous *Herball* was published in 1633 fifty species of Mediterranean and European orchids were known.

The first western reference to an exotic species is found in an Aztec herbal of 1552, the Badianus MS, in which the Vanilla is illustrated. This was also the first tropical orchid to be named, for at the beginning of the next century the botanist and traveller Charles Lecluse called it *Lobus oblongus aromaticus*.

Tropical orchids from Asia are first described by H. A. Reede tot Draakenstein who was appointed governor of the Dutch island of Malabar during the second half of the seventeenth century. The formation of the Dutch East India Company and its establishment of trading posts throughout the Far East made possible the gathering of much valuable information on local flora and fauna. For example, Engelbert Kaempfer, a brilliant and tireless German doctor who was sent to Batavia (now Djakarta) in Java and later to Japan, made drawings as well as copious notes and published his work in 1712. It contained three illustrations of orchids, one of which was *Dendrobium moniliforme*.

The botanical interest in orchids progressed gradually but gained increasing momentum as more knowledge became available and the improvement in microscopy made really detailed observation possible. It is probable that, but for the invention of the achromatic lens by Chestermoor Hall in 1729, taxonomy or plant physiology would have advanced very little after the beginning of the eighteenth century. Prior to this the distortion of both colour and shape rendered the microscope more of a curious toy than a precise scientific instrument. After John Dolland had worked on improving the lens from 1752 to 1757 Lister adapted it to the microscope, thus opening the door to a wide variety of scientists, including of course the taxonomist.

The work of the taxonomists and botanists, the history of their gradual classification of the family Orchidaceae and their discovery of its methods of fertilization and reproduction, are discussed in detail in chapter two; it is difficult to visualize the state in which present-day orchid growing would be, worldwide as it is, without their contribution.

From the beginning of the nineteenth century the number of tropical orchids finding their way back to England gradually increased, sent back by botanists and travellers or brought home by seamen putting in at distant ports. As more and more specimens were seen by the public the beauty and strangeness of the flowers created great excitement, and a growing demand to own specimens of these rare and exotic blooms brought into being the great nurseries whose names are now classics in the world of orchids. One of the earliest and most famous was James Veitch and Sons. James Veitch owned a general plant nursery in Exeter

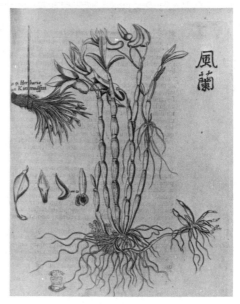

Dendrobium moniliforme, previously called *Epidendrum moniliforme* and one of the first orchids to which there is a written reference, is a native of Japan. This drawing is taken from the account of his travels which Engelbert Kaempfer published in 1712.

Right: The five Veitchs, who pioneered the collection and later the hybridization of orchids

James Veitch.
James H. Veitch.
James Veitch, junior.
John Veitch.
Harry J. Veitch.

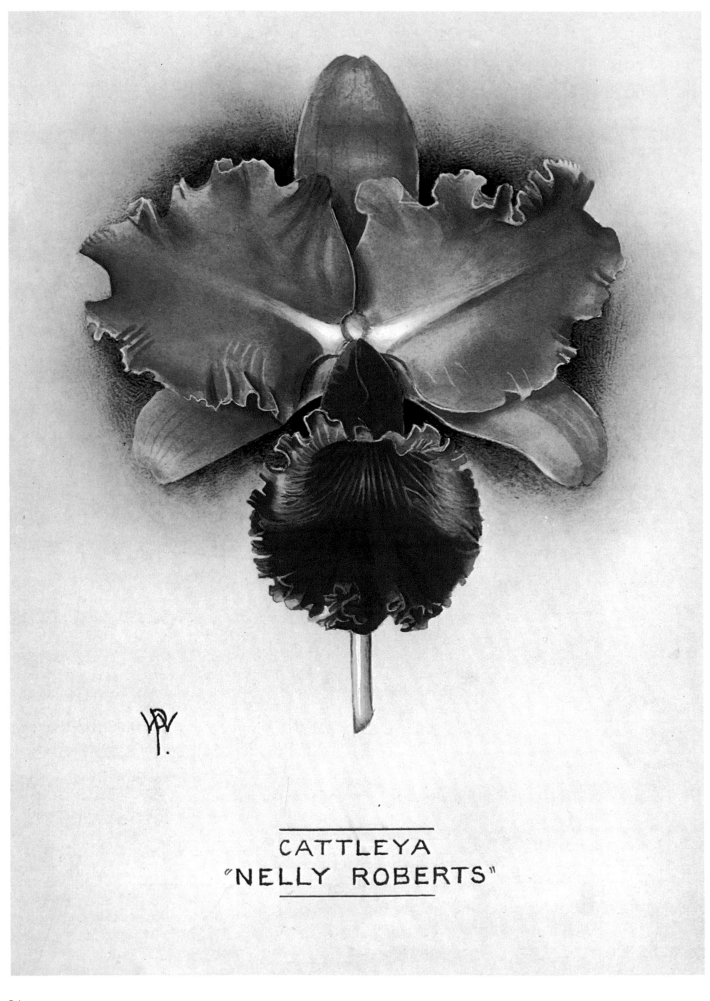

CATTLEYA
"NELLY ROBERTS"

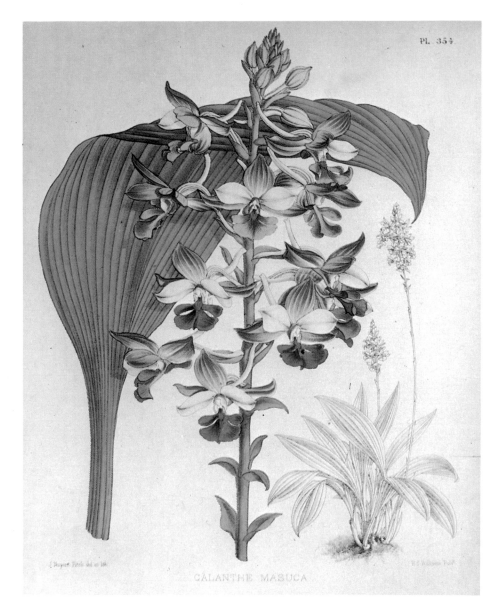

PL. 354.

CALANTHE MASUCA

'justly regarded as the finest of the kind ever known in England' from which plant collectors were sent as far as Brazil and Japan, but it was when he moved to Chelsea to take possession of the old-established firm of Knight and Perry–the Royal Exotic Nursery–in 1853, and in the same year it was discovered by one of his gardeners that the hybridization of orchids was possible, that the greatest period of the orchid section of the firm began.

Up to the middle of the nineteenth century the hybridization of orchids had been thought to be an impossibility. One collector even explained his enthusiasm for the species 'because those fiends the hybridizers cannot get at them'. It was John Dominy, a relatively untutored Scots gardener who was described as the 'devoted and faithful servant and friend' of James Veitch, who first achieved success. In 1853, having been initiated in to the mysteries of the reproductive system in orchids by Mr John Harris of Exeter–a surgeon with botanical training–he fertilized *Calanthe masuca* with *C. furcata* and this cross, or 'orchidaceous mule' as the Victorians termed it, produced its first flowers in 1856. From then on it became possible to breed selectively for colour, size, shape and any other characteristic desired; the hybridists have worked so assiduously since that there are now over 45,000 registered hybrids.

15

By the latter years of the nineteenth century Frederick Sander's name was world famous among orchid lovers. He had nurseries both in Belgium and England and included many of the royal houses of Europe among his clients. In the small picture Leopold II, King of the Belgians, is in conversation with Frederick

Sander (left) at the 1901 summer show of the Belgian Royal Society of Gardeners and Fruit Growers. On the right is a group photograph taken in 1897 of his orchid collectors, nursery staff and student apprentices in Bruges. Mrs Sander stands in the centre of the balcony with their son Fearnly and his wife.

17

In addition to working on the creation of new hybrids there was a continued search for new species in their natural habitat. Great competition developed between rival orchid establishments and collectors were sent all over the world, often at great personal risk, to track down rare orchids. Owing to the difficulty orchid growers experienced in reproducing new stock from seed, enormous numbers of plants were sent home; one collector reported that he had packed up 17,000 specimens of one particular species, *Cattleya rex,* while another, after he had gathered as many plants of one orchid as he could take with him, destroyed all others of the same species he could find to preserve its rarity. Nowadays there are regulations prohibiting the massive export of orchids in most countries to which they are native. The giant among nineteenth-century orchid hunters was Frederick Sander, whose teams of collectors were sent to all parts of the world, and whose name is commemorated in countless species and hybrids.

The huge volume of literature published about orchids up to the beginning of this century has been, in great part, written by scientists for reading by scientists. Although many of the wealthy amateurs, the builders of the great collections of the nineteenth century, were cultured and informed orchidists, their field was in the acquisition of fine forms of varieties of the torrent of species imported from different parts of the tropical world. For example, the records show that the Royal Horticultural Society granted fifty-six First Class Certificates and Awards of Merit to *Cattleya mossiae* up to 1935, thirty-seven of which went to amateur exhibitors. The first was given in 1865.

A different form of works on orchids was inevitable, written by cultivators of these plants and giving instructions on the different requirements of the great numbers of species. When orchids were first imported into northern Europe in significant quantities towards the end of the eighteenth century, little was known of their needs in captivity. They were introduced by seamen or other non-botanists and were immediately put into 'stoves' or hot houses heated by a bricked flue underneath the house. This method of heating dried out the inside of the hothouse and consequently vast quantities of water were used to counteract the aridity and to keep the heat as much under control as possible. The result was an atmosphere something between that of a Turkish bath and an old-fashioned London fog and, not surprisingly, most plants died soon after their arrival. Of all the means devised by man for the destruction of orchid plants this must be one of the most efficient. As one early enthusiast lamented 'I had caught my orchid but how to treat it I knew not'.

It was only the coming of cast iron and the use of four and six inch cast iron pipes, water-filled and heated by a boiler, that made the long-term cultivation of greenhouse plants possible. Even then, and for many years to follow, the cooler-growing orchids did not thrive. After a time, however, it was realized that although the orchids brought home were tropical in origin, not all were used to a hot, steamy Amazonic atmosphere, and when the growers ceased to be afraid of allowing fresh air into their orchid houses, success quickly followed.

In a book published in 1893, *Orchids : Their Culture and Management with Descriptions of all the kinds in General Cultivation,* by W. Watson and W. Bean, the following excerpt from the

This stove house constructed by Mr Dillwyn Llewellyn, from *The Gardeners' Chronicle*, 1850, shows the expense to which the Victorians were prepared to go in pursuit of their hobby. As well as looking more natural the waterfall raised the humidity and gave a fresh feeling to the atmosphere.

Right: Mr Bull's *Odontoglossum* house in 1881. The plants on the bench would now be called miltonias, while the odontoglossums are growing on rafts hanging from the roof.

section on 'the treatment of newly imported orchids' gives a little idea of what orchid plants had to suffer before arriving at the refuge of their future home: 'The peculiar condition under which Orchids are found wild, the manner in which they are collected, and conveyed long distances in boxes, etc. by mule, boat and steamer, together with the radical change they necessarily are compelled to undergo before they are established in gardens here, render their treatment on first arrival very important. Thousands of plants are sold weekly, at the auction-rooms and elsewhere, which are either immediately killed, or irrecoverably weakened by wrong treatment at the outset. As a rule, the roots of newly-imported plants are all dead, and few, if any, leaves remain on such as Odontoglossums, Dendrobiums, etc., although the pseudo-bulbs may be sound enough'.

Perhaps the most popular and ambitious of the more modest publications was *The Orchid Grower's Manual* by B. S. Williams, 1894. To have some idea of the number of publications to do with orchids at that date, one has only to look at his 'List of Illustrated Botanical Works Referred To In This Book'. There are 109, the earliest dated 1733–1743, finishing with *A Manual of Orchidaceous Plants,* 1894.

All these books helped to create a growing interest in orchids

and orchid culture among a wider public. Periodicals such as *The Gardeners' Chronicle* contained illustrated articles about orchids and *The Orchid Review,* a specialist monthly publication, was started in 1893 by R. A. Rolfe. It is still a vigorous publication,

Paphiopedilum charlesworthii, painted by R. A.
Rolfe, formed the frontispiece to the first
edition of *The Orchid Review* published in
1893

having survived two world wars. The first issue, Vol. 1. No. 1, of
January 1893 includes a quotation from Charles Darwin, 'It is
interesting to look at one of the magnificent exotic species, or,
indeed, at one of our humblest forms, and observe how pro-
foundly it has been modified, as compared with all ordinary
flowers'.

This first issue contained several interesting items. There was,
for instance, the first part of a series of articles on orchid
hybridization, which was presumably written by the editor, who
later produced the fore-runner of *Sander's List of Orchid
Hybrids, The Orchid Stud-Book,* in collaboration with C. C.
Hurst. There were articles on various new and unusual species
and a review of the awards given by the Royal Horticultural
Society during the year 1892. Veitch and Sons of Chelsea were
easily in the lead with seven First Class Certificates and eleven
Awards of Merit. A report on the dozen orchid houses of the
Burford collection required five and a half pages to describe the
various fine hybrids and species.

This collection belonged to Sir Trevor Lawrence, the president
of the Royal Horticultural Society. Large specimen plants, the
result of having plenty of time and patience, were the vogue in
the late 1890s. In a group shown by Sir Trevor at the last R.H.S.
meeting of the year was a pan of *Sophronitis grandiflora ;* it con-

tained a single plant fourteen inches in diameter, with over forty flowers. It was awarded a Silver Banksian Medal, nowadays given only to groups–perhaps the judges thought this pan *was* a group. At the same meeting C. E. Smith of Cobham showed a single specimen of *Cypripedium insigne* with ninety-six blooms, all of first-class size and colouring. Exhibitors from all parts of the country, both amateur and trade growers, sent plants and there was also one entry from Brussels.

Two books of great significance to the orchid world appeared in 1906; one was, in a way, a summing up of progress to the date of publication, and the other a very different work which had an immediate influence on orchid growing, an influence which has continued and increased with the passing of the years. The first was *Hortus Veitchii* by James H. Veitch and was a record of the history of the firm of James Veitch and Sons, their many triumphs and accomplishments and also their disasters. It contained a valuable list of their hybrids and importations of species covering all branches of horticulture including the orchid.

The other book, *Sander's List of Orchid Hybrids,* although it, too, recorded the achievements of the past, was far more forward-looking. F. W. Burbidge, who later became one of the most distinguished of Veitch's collectors in Borneo, had attempted a hybrid list in 1871 which contained seventeen crosses, although it was only fifteen years after the first hybrid had flowered for John Dominy in Veitch's nursery. *Sander's List* was an up-to-date list of all the known hybrids and the first efficient attempt to bring order out of a confusion which was certain to become more chaotic. Addenda were published regularly, allowing for the two world wars, the latest taking the list to January, 1971. In 1961 the work of revision was undertaken by the International Registrar of Orchid Cultivars. This list is vital especially to the smooth running of an orchid breeder's life, although it is not a stud book as clonal or varietal names of parents are not registered because of the enormous amount of space this would require. The late F. K. Sander, the originator to whom the orchid world will be indebted forever, wished to simplify the list and not to complicate it further.

In addition to the *List,* Sanders produced another book essential to orchid enthusiasts–and more particularly to the practical ones who are growers–*Sander's Orchid Guide ;* this was first published in 1901, the latest edition being dated 1925. This book gives cultural directions in great detail, and then specific cultural instructions at the beginning of each generic section, together with an account of distribution and of variations in the range of species. This is followed by a very detailed description of individual species with suggested variations in treatment for the culture of each.

Although the many books were of great importance, the greatest influence in arousing interest in orchids during the nineteenth century, the century of the beginning of understanding of orchid culture and of orchid hybridization, was undoubtedly the Horticultural Society, which became the Royal Horticultural Society in 1861. The Society's rise in influence on all gardening matters was parallel to the growth of interest in orchids. Many of its presidents have, in fact, been eminent in one branch or other of orchidology.

The monthly meetings, which the general public could also attend on payment of an entrance fee, enabled many thousands of citizens to see the best of specimen plants on display. In the case of orchids, these specimens were at first selected from the constant flow of fresh importations but after the discovery that orchids could be hybridized by man an increasing number of hybrids was exhibited.

The Orchid Committee, formed in 1889, was, and still is, empowered to recommend to the R.H.S. Council that a plant placed before it for its appraisal be granted, in order of importance, a Preliminary Commendation, an Award of Merit or a First Class Certificate. There is also a Cultural Commendation for exceptionally well-grown plants. To gain an Award of Merit an orchid must gain twice as many votes for as against it, and three times as many for a First Class Certificate; a painting is then made of all plants granted these awards and also of those gaining a Preliminary Commendation. Since 1897 copies of paintings have been filed in the Orchid Room and the relevant painting is produced for comparison purposes if a hybrid plant having the same parentage as a hybrid already granted an award is placed before the Committee.

The first artist officially commissioned by the R.H.S. was Miss Nellie Roberts. It is said that when a girl of seventeen she saw a vase of orchids in a window in Camberwell, where she lived, and was so entranced by their beauty that she asked the owner if she might be allowed to paint them. These were the first orchids she painted in a career lasting nearly sixty years. Owing to her unique occupation she had the keenest of eyes for an orchid, for the blooms had to be reproduced with meticulous accuracy for their function of comparison. *Cattleya* Nellie Roberts was named for her during her lifetime. When she was presented with a painting by another artist of the first of this hybrid to flower she remarked, after giving her thanks, that she would have preferred to have painted it herself.

As well as having the opportunity to examine orchids at meetings of the R.H.S., the public was also able to see orchids in cultivation at the Royal Botanic Gardens at Kew, near London. Here visitors were allowed to stroll through the various greenhouses, some of which were devoted entirely to orchids. At present, although there are numerous species, very few—if any—hybrids are cultivated there, but it is still the training ground for some of the foremost orchidists.

Although what might almost be termed the great Age of Orchids came to an end in 1914, interest in orchids—and particularly in the raising of hybrids—has continued to increase, greatly helped, of course, by the discovery first of the asymbiotic method of germinating orchid seed and, after the Second World War, of a way of reproducing orchid plants by the propagation of meristem tissue. An indication of how this interest has spread, not only in Britain but in every part of the world, is the number of orchid societies which has proliferated in recent years. In England, for example, there was only one orchid society before 1939, The Manchester and North of England Society; now there are dozens, headed by the Orchid Society of Great Britain, which issues its own *Journal*. A further influence in the popularizing of orchids was the formation of the British Orchid Growers'

An early meeting of the Orchid Committee of the R.H.S. The assistant is displaying a painting with his left hand and holding up the plant, a cattleya, with his right. In the background the majority of plants for assessment seem to be odontoglossums—there seems to be more variation in the headgear than in the orchids.

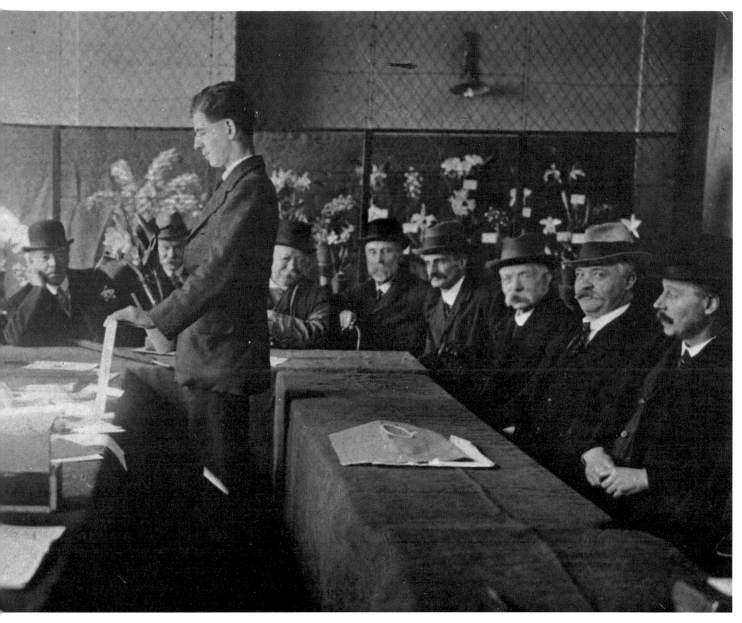

Association in 1948. Although purely a trade association, the B.O.G.A. started to organize annual orchid shows with considerable co-operation from the R.H.S. The Third World Orchid Conference was held in 1960 and was sponsored jointly by the American Orchid Society, the B.O.G.A. and the R.H.S. It attracted orchid enthusiasts and exhibits from all over the world, one of the most decorative groups being that of the Malaysian Orchid Society for which a Gold Medal was awarded.

The American Orchid Society was formed in 1921 by amateur, private and commercial growers, and from a membership of less than a 100 has grown to over 13,000. It is the focal point for many clubs and societies not only in North America but throughout the world. The monthly *Bulletin* is full of useful information gained from practical experience, scientific articles and notes from affiliated societies – in fact, something for everyone.

There are orchid societies in many other parts of the world and all, both the large and the not so large, are full of enthusiasm and eager to communicate their knowledge and experience of growing orchids to any newcomer willing to learn. To join one is to become a member of an enormous family.

The family Orchidaceae

All plants belong to various families distinguished from each other by differences in the structure of their flowers, stems, leaves and roots. Each family is split up into tribes, or a number of main divisions, and each tribe is further split up into genera, or the main divisions of the tribe. These divisions are established by similarities in the appearance and construction of the flowers, each genus being further divided into smaller groups with even greater similarities which are called species. This system of classification has been established after centuries of hard work and investigation by taxonomists and other botanical scientists, particularly during the last 150 years since the advent of the microscope. Orchids of all kinds belong to the family Orchidaceae which is one of the largest families of flowering plants, containing almost one seventh of all those on earth. It is made up of nearly 1,000 different genera and probably about 20,000 species.

It would be far beyond the scope of this book to attempt to deal with more than a few of the genera, nor would it be of much practical advantage to the reader, for vast numbers of orchids – although undoubtedly of high botanical and scientific interest – are so small as to be appreciated only under a strong magnifying glass by the initiated. Some, indeed, are so tiny that a complete plant would fit easily into a thimble, the flowers being no more than the size of pinheads, while others have flowering stems fifteen to twenty feet long.

All orchids, whether they are the native European species or tropical exotics found in the steamy jungles of the Amazon or on the lower slopes of the Himalayas, have a family likeness in that they all share certain characteristics which differentiate them from all other families of flowering plants. All orchids have three sepals and these frequently conform to the colour of the petals, of which there are also three; in some species these parts may be fused or reduced. One of the petals in the orchid is always dif-

ferent from the others, often larger and more brilliantly coloured or patterned, and takes the form of a lip or labellum, a tube, a pouch or one of several other variations. Projecting from the centre of the flower is a member called the column which contains both the male and female reproductive organs. This fusion is characteristic of an orchid as in most other flowers the male and female sexual organs are separate. The anther at the top of the column contains the pollen—in many genera this is grouped in two to eight coherent sticky masses called pollinia—and immediately below it is the stigmatic surface (the female section of the column) on which the pollinia must be deposited during fertilization. After this has taken place the ovary at the base of the column develops into a seed capsule or pod which may contain as many as a million seeds. These are so small that to the naked eye they look like a fine powder.

Although all orchids have these characteristics in common, there are very great differences between genera and species—in shape, size, colour, manner of growth and habitat. During the course of evolution orchids have adapted themselves in many different ways to their diverse environments. Although all are perennial they may be epiphytic or terrestrial, lithophytic or saprophytic, but no species is parasitic as is sometimes popularly believed.

Typical Amazon country, the type of jungle habitat in which many tropical species are found

An *Aerangis* species from tropical Africa.
Note the very long spur attached to the base
of the labellum, one of the many modifications
of the third petal.

Epiphytes grow on trees, sometimes very high up to reach the
light and air. They send out long tough aerial roots the main
function of which is to anchor the plant to the host tree. These
roots have a thick white parchment-like wall, only the half-inch
growing tip being green, and often have thick short hairs which
adhere to the tree or the branch on which the plant is perched.
Nourishment is absorbed mainly through the leaves in the form
of minute particles of organic matter. Lithophytes have a similar
mode of growth but attach themselves to rocks, while saprophytic
species are practically rootless and leafless and feed on dead
organic matter. The terrestrial species, amongst which are almost
all European orchids, draw their nourishment directly from the
soil in which they grow.

The progress to our present knowledge of the Orchidaceae was
gradual, however. Although orchid classification had its origins in
the listing of southern European species by the ancient Greeks
and the plant catalogues of mediaeval herbalists, it was first put
on a scientific basis by the work of Carl Linnaeus, 'the founder
of modern botany', in the eighteenth century. His system was
based on differences in sexual characters and followed the binary

Masdevallia harryana coerulescens shows yet another strange orchid shape. The genus *Masdevallia* is native to Central and South America.

method of naming plants, that is the genus was named first and then the species. For example, a modern equivalent would be *Cattleya* (genus) *dowiana* (species). In *Species Plantarum*, which was published in 1743, he named eight genera and sixty species of orchids.

Linnaeus visited Paris in 1758–9 and met the famous de Jussieu family. Bernard de Jussieu, later Superintendent of the gardens of the Petit Trianon, worked out a method of arranging plants systematically and his nephew Antoine Laurent extended this system and published *Genera Plantarum* – the foundation of modern botanical classification – in 1789.

A further significant contribution to orchid knowledge at that time was made by Oloff Swartz, one of Linnaeus's successors in the Chair of Botany at Upsala. After a detailed investigation into the floral parts of orchids, he separated them into two main divisions, those with two anthers (most orchids) and those with one, the genus *Cypripedium*. These two divisions were later adopted by Lindley under the names Diandrous and Monandrous.

It was not until the beginning of the nineteenth century that the principles of the classification of the Orchidaceae were really

Left: A splendid illustration of epiphytes in their natural setting; there are many other plants in this community in addition to several species of orchid.

Above: Platanthera bifolia, a terrestrial species found from northern Asia to China as well as in Europe. Some of the 250 species in this genus grow in tropical Africa and South America.

Neottia nidus-avis, the Bird's Nest Orchid. It was from the matted, bird's nest-like roots of this saprophytic species that symbiosis was first discovered in the orchid family.

put on a solid basis. In 1801 a young Scot called Robert Brown joined Captain Flinders's expedition to survey the Australian coastline as a botanist. He returned home with the expedition in 1805 with 4,000 species of Australian plants, many of which were new to science, and later published *Prodromus Florae Novae Hollandae et Insulae Van Diemens*. His adoption, with modifications, of the natural system of de Jussieu led to its general use in place of the Linnean method.

The most eminent scientific orchid botanist of the nineteenth century, however, was John Lindley. Unlike so many of his predecessors he was the son of a nurseryman, and in 1822 was appointed Assistant Secretary of the Horticultural Society and in 1829 Professor of Botany at London University, a post he held until 1860. Following on from Brown, Lindley worked out, chiefly in the *Botanical Register* which he edited for many years, the systematic arrangement of species which has supplied the foundation of every subsequent classification.

The Genera and Species of Orchidaceous Plants took ten years of preparation during which time so many more species of the three principal tribes described were discovered that a Revision of the

Linnaeus, the 'father of modern botany'

Right: Bull's catalogue cover for 1898 showing a spray of *Odontoglossum crispum*; most of the orchids offered inside are species. In the latter half of the nineteenth century the interest in species stimulated a constant search for new treasures and brought many unkown orchids to the attention of the taxonomists.

Order was indispensable. The volumes contain Latin descriptions of 1,980 species with occasional notes in English. Lindley worked from dried specimens – and sometimes live plants – he received from many parts of the world and the following list of some of his sources demonstrates the wide distribution of the family of orchids: Europe, Siberia, North Africa, northern U.S.A., Canada, California, Texas, Carolina, Mexico, Central America, Peru, Brazil, Chile, the West Indies, Guyana, Madeira, tropical Africa, Madagascar, Cape of Good Hope, Malaya, Ceylon, Burma, the Himalayas, Assam, China ('but of that country and Japan very little can be said to be known'), Tasmania and Australia. The Orchidaceae of Java, Sumatra, the Philippines and the eastern and northern coasts of Australia were relatively unknown at that time. The work was completed in 1840, and twelve years after the publication of the last of its parts Lindley started on the revision and re-systemization of many of the genera.

After Lindley's monumental labours a great many publications on the classification of orchids regularly appeared, the early ones based on Lindley's system, but altering or modifying it as or when new species or genera, some of which were thought to be missing links and some of which confirmed opinions or guesses, were discovered.

There had been a rapid growth of interest in orchids as more and more tropical species were seen and gardeners gradually discovered how to achieve success in keeping plants alive and producing flowers on them. Commercial nurseries and orchid growers started to cater for the increasing demand for these exotic plants and this commercial interest gave great impetus to the growth in knowledge of the Orchidaceae. Although in 1826 the Horticultural Society had been proud to record that 'by singular exertion' it had 'succeeded in two years in forming such a collection of this tribe of curious plants as was never seen in Europe before. It consists of about 180 tropical kinds', little more than ten years later James Bateman, speaking of 1837, was able to note 'not less, probably, than three hundred species were seen in England for the first time in this memorable year'. The number of species known to science continued to increase with even greater rapidity as the first orchid hunters were sent by rival firms to remote and sometimes virtually unexplored territories in search of new treasures, and many growers co-operated closely with plant physiologists and taxonomists. For example, Reichenbach, a close friend of Lindley and of Sander, produced three volumes in which numerous previously unknown species were described and illustrated. They were published by Frederick Sander in the latter half of the nineteenth century and contained many species first discovered by his own collectors.

As more and more knowledge on the Orchidaceae has been accumulated, many more specialized books have appeared, sometimes devoted to an individual genus or group of genera or sometimes to the orchids indigenous to a particular continent, country or type of habitat.

Orchids grow in a wider range of habitats than almost any other family of plants. Their distribution is worldwide and they can be found in climates ranging from the arctic to the tropical, but the abundance and variety of species is by far the greatest in

ENTERED AT STATIONERS HALL

1898.

Nº 324.

A List of

By Special Appointment

New, Rare & Beautiful

PLANTS AND ORCHIDS

OFFERED BY WILLIAM BULL, F.L.S.

F.R.G.S. F.Z.S. F.R.H.S. M.A.I. F.R.B.S. & M.S.A.

Socc. Hort. Berol. Bruxell. St Petersburgh et Paris et Soc. Agric. et Bot. Gandav. Socius.

New Plant Merchant.

536, KING'S ROAD, CHELSEA, LONDON, S.W.

Epiphytes in Assam; the anchoring roots and seed capsules can be clearly seen in this picture.

the tropical belts of both the Old and the New Worlds. It has been reported that up to fifty different species have been found growing among the ferns, bromeliads, begonias and other epiphytes on a single felled tree in Venezuela. Although orchids are most common at heights of 1,500 to 5,000 feet, they also flourish at 14,000 feet in the Andes and at sea level and one Australian genus with only one species, *Rhizanthella gardneri*, grows and flowers completely underground.

Most of the tropical and subtropical species are epiphytic, often growing as much as 100 feet above ground in the tree tops of the cloud and rain forests in their struggle for light and air. In semi-desert areas such species as *Oncidium onustum* are epiphytic on cacti, and there are even some epiphytes—*Epidendrum boothianum* of the Florida Keys, for example—which can survive the drying effects of the salt conditions prevailing in mangrove swamps. Many orchids have special adaptations to counteract the harshness of their environment. For instance, those which are subjected to long periods of drought have pseudobulbs which act as water storage organs to help them through the dry period; in cultivation they need an extended rest (dry) period to flower properly.

Most temperate climate species are terrestrial, being found in a variety of conditions ranging from sunny grassy pastures—as are many species of the genus *Orchis*, for example – to wet meadows and bogs. The Dune Helleborine (*Epipactis dunensis*) is even found growing among the sand dunes of the beaches of western and northern Europe.

Some genera such as *Habenaria* and *Spiranthes* are worldwide with species in both temperate and tropical climates, although distribution may be local within this wide area, while others are limited to certain geographic regions. *Cattleya* is restricted to Central and South America, for example, while *Vanda* and *Dendrobium* are found only in Asia and Australasia. Some genera have a more restricted distribution, however, such as *Eulophiella* which grows only in Madagascar.

Perhaps the genera which are of greatest interest to the grower are those which are most readily cultivated in glasshouses and which in consequence have become what are generally called commercial orchids. There are four main ones: *Cattleya, Odontoglossum, Cymbidium* and *Paphiopedilum*. These are the genera which have attracted the attention of the hybridizer and which form the major part of the greenhouse orchid population in many parts of the world. In addition there are many other genera which are cultivated in fewer numbers but which are also very showy and rewarding orchids to grow, such as *Dendrobium, Oncidium,* and *Epidendrum*. At present *Phalaenopsis* is becoming very popular and much hybridization is being carried out in Malaysia, Hawaii and mainland U.S.A. A particular genus of orchid is usually cultivated in the climate best suited to it and this is the reason why the heat- and humidity-loving genera such as *Aranda, Vanda,* and *Arachnis* are so prolifically grown and hybridized in Malaysia and not in temperate climates. Most of the orchids grown there are cultivated in the open air and heating is not the problem – nor the expense – it is in cooler countries.

The *Cattleya* genus is named after the botanist William Cattley, who was a friend of Sir Joseph Banks and specialized in collecting cattleyas as a hobby. It is Central and South American in origin and contains nearly seventy species, all of which are epiphytic with prominent pseudobulbs from four inches to four feet in height. The flowers are often very large with the third petal modified into a lip or labellum, usually but not always with a fringed edge. The basal part (that which is joined to the rest of the flower) is usually in the form of a tube, and the column is enclosed in this tube. The cattleyas, because of the structure of their flowers, are allied to many other genera which they resemble in appearance, and inter-breeding between these allied genera has produced many more beautiful forms than would have been possible by adhering to one genus only. Many intergeneric hybrids have the appearance of a cattleya and it is only by investigating the reproductive parts of the flowers that the differences become clear. The genera most usually crossed in the alliance are *Cattleya, Laelia, Sophronitis* (although the tiny *Sophronitis grandiflora,* the species used many generations ago, has not often been reintroduced owing to the reduction in size of the progeny) and *Brassavola*. Other allied genera such as *Epidendrum* have also been used and work is at present going on in an attempt to bring new forms into use.

The naming of orchids, especially of intergeneric hybrids, has posed problems in the past. When a *Cattleya* species is crossed with a *Laelia* the result is a *Laeliocattleya*. If this is crossed with

Habenaria susannae, a very showy member of a genus with a practically wordwide distribution which was awarded a Certificate by the Orchid Committee of the R.H.S. as early as 1894

33

A selection of orchids native to Western Australia

Right: Oncidium pusillum is an example of one of the very small-growing orchids. Others are so tiny that they would actually fit inside the thimble.

Below: *Aerangis friesiorum* is an epiphytic, tropical African species.

Dendrobium lituiflorum, an example of a lithophytic or rock-growing species.

Graceful, arching spikes of modern hybrid
Odontoglossum and allied genera, a result of
generations of selective breeding

Right: Miltonia spectabilis, one of the Brazilian
species, distinct from the Colombian in form
and in the deeper green of the foliage

a *Sophronitis* the result is a *Sophrolaeliocattleya.* If, however, this is in turn crossed with a *Brassavola* the addition of the name of this genus to the three already mentioned would produce so cumbersome and uneuphonious a name that, for the sake of brevity, this quadrigeneric hybrid, the result of crossing four genera, is called a *Potinara,* after a great French amateur grower of the past M. Felix Potin. The first potinaras, made from crosses between these four genera, were registered in 1923.

There are two kinds of cattleyas, the most numerous at present being the labiata or unifoliate type. These are called after *Cattleya labiata,* the first species to be discovered. This has two, three or more very large flowers, usually with a fringed labellum, and the leaves are arranged on the pseudobulbs singly. This type of cattleya is found mostly in Colombia and Brazil, and it is because of its wide distribution that the various members of this group have different flowering periods. For instance, *C. trianae* from Colombia flowers during the winter, *C. warneri* from Brazil is a summer bloomer, and *C. schroederae,* another Colombian, flowers in the spring. The other type is bifoliate, the leaves being arranged on the pseudobulb in pairs. The flowers of this group are smaller and more numerous than in the labiata group, but because hybridizing – although increasing in recent years – was neglected in the past, there are consequently fewer bifoliate hybrids.

The *Odontoglossum* genus – so named from the Greek words for 'tooth' and 'tongue' in reference to the tooth-like projections on the lip – is distributed over a very wide area comprising the mountains of Peru, Colombia (where the majority of species is found), Mexico, Brazil, Guatemala, Costa Rica, Panama, Honduras and Nicaragua. The genus is epiphytic and most species are found very high up – at 10,000 feet and more – in the Andes and other mountain ranges.

The flowers of odontoglossums are numerous on the flower spikes but variable in size and relatively few of the 300 or so species have been used in hybridizing. The lip is like an apron and the column free-standing. As with *Cattleya,* there are numerous allied genera which interbreed readily with *Odontoglossum* and modern hybrids are especially attractive owing to the infusion of red from *Cochlioda* and to their larger size from the introduction of *Miltonia.* The species used most in hybridizing is the magnificent *O. crispum* with large white flowers, often spotted or suffused with rose, and a bright golden lip, and the largest species is the noble *O. grande* with six-inch-wide yellow flowers striped with red-brown bars, a truly dramatic orchid.

The genus *Miltonia* is a very attractive one, with large flat brilliantly coloured blooms in sprays of five to a dozen flowers each; it is sometimes regarded as a warmer-growing odontoglossum and was, indeed, originally classified as such. There are about thirty species found in Colombia, Brazil, Costa Rica and Peru. They are epiphytes and grow at altitudes of from 1,000 to 6,000 feet. The remarkable thing about the huge modern hybrids is that they are mostly the result of breeding from only two species, both Colombian, *M. vexillaria* and *M. roezlii,* but another Colombian species *M. phalaenopsis* has sometimes been used as well. This gives an infusion of pale rose to some of the hybrids. The Brazilian species, of which *M. spectabilis* and its

Cattleya labiata, the type after which
the large and preponderant group of cattleyas
is named

Left: The curiously patterned *Odontoglossum* hybrid Florence Stirling

Below: Cattleya mossiae has many varieties, one of the most famous being *wagnerii*, used very extensively to obtain white cattleyas; the species has produced many fine mauve hybrids.

Paphiopedilum callosum, a typical species of the tessellated foliage group in this genus. The tip of the ventral sepal can be seen just below the labellum.

variants are the most spectacular (owing to their brilliant red and purple colouring), are different in form and in the colour of their foliage. Miltonias flower in May and June when other orchid blooms are scarce but their disadvantage is that the flowers do not last when cut.

Cymbidium also derives its name from Greek, from the word for a boat because of the boat-shaped hollow recess in the labellum. The genus is distributed over a vast area of the Far East including northern India, Burma, Annam, Korea, Japan, China, New Guinea and the Philippines. The first plant of this genus to be imported into England was *C. pendulum* from India, at the end of the eighteenth century, and there are now about seventy recorded species. Whereas cattleyas and odontoglossums are solely epiphytes, some cymbidiums are terrestrial or lithophytic (rock-dwellers). The vast majority are found growing at heights of from 1,000 to over 5,000 feet above sea level but the average is 5,000 feet. The flowers appear on a spike starting from the base of the pseudobulb and are very numerous, especially in some of the hybrids. *Cymbidium* is the most popular orchid genus in production today, and more crossing has been done in recent years than in any other genus in England. Although there are more than sixty species, only a few have been selected by hybridizers for the production of the many thousands of different hybrids in collections all over the world. The flowers are large and fleshy and cover a wide range of colours from white to flushed rose and deep red, from the palest to the deepest green and cream to brilliant yellow—a tremendous advance from the dowdy browns and russets of a century ago. The column, like that in *Odontoglossum,* is free-standing and the lip can be narrow or quite wide and of a contrasting colour to the sepals and petals. The leaves are long and usually narrow.

The tropical genus *Paphiopedilum* (formerly misnamed *Cypripedium*) is popularly known as Lady's Slipper or Slipper of Venus because of its shoe-shaped pouch. It is possibly the most curious of the genera described here owing to the shape of its flowers and to various structural differences between it and all other orchids. Paphiopedilums are found in most parts of Asia—particularly north-eastern India and Burma—both at altitudes of 5,000 to 6,000 feet and almost at sea level. The atmosphere is always moist and, even at the maximum heights, quite warm at all times. Most species are terrestrial, although a few grow in trees and some lithophytic types are occasionally found growing on limestone rocks.

There are no pseudobulbs in *Paphiopedilum* and usually there is one flower to a stem and this rises from the middle of the new growth, but there are one or two exceptions to this rule, some species having three or four flowers. The flower is unusual in that it appears to have only two sepals instead of the usual three because, during the course of evolution, two have fused together to form the ventral (lower) sepal. This connate sepal sometimes shows its ancestry by becoming bifurcated in some hybrids, a trait which is considered a stigma by judges. The labellum is in the form of a pouch and whereas all other genera of orchids have only one fertile anther a *Paphiopedilum* species has two. The distinguishing features of a modern *Paphiopedilum* hybrid are the great dorsal (upper) sepal and wide petals together with a brilliant coloration seldom seen in the species.

The genus *Phalaenopsis* (so called because of the resemblance of the bloom to a moth) is widely distributed throughout the equatorial zone of the Far East; many of the most showy and attractive species are found in the Philippines in places which have a high temperature and a high humidity.

Blume named the genus from a specimen of the pure white *P. amabalis* which he had found on the island of Nusa Kambangu, and published his description in 1825. Prior to this, however, the species had passed through many nomenclatural adventures. It was first discovered by Rumphius on the island of Amboina and described and illustrated by him in 1750 under the name *Angraecum album majus;* in *Species Plantarum,* 1753, Linnaeus noted dried specimens sent to him from Java as *Epidendrum amabile;* while in 1798 more plants, discovered in the Moluccas and sent to the East India Company's botanic garden at Calcutta, were described by Dr Roxburgh in his *Flora Indica* under the genus *Cymbidium.* Even as late as 1847 John Lindley, on seeing the flower of a plant sent back from Java by Thomas Lobb, gave it the name *Phalaenopsis grandiflora.* It is found in various parts

Vanda rothschildiana, a primary hybrid between *V. coerulea* and *V. sanderiana*, shows a hint of the colour of its pod parent, *V. coerulea*.

Below: Phalaenopsis amabilis, introduced by Thomas Lobb in 1846

Far left: Cymbidium Brigadoon Lewes, a delightful flower with contrasting labellum and other segments and the desirable round shape or form. These, together with an arching spike, make this cymbidium very appealing.

of the Malayan Archipelago, sometimes close to the seashore almost within reach of the spray, sometimes high in the branches of trees.

Apart from the natural hybrids, such as *P. intermedia,* there are now many hundreds of hybrids within the genus but, more significantly, it has been interbred with other genera – *Vanda, Doritis, Renanthera, Arachnis* and *Aerides* have all been used – to produce intergeneric hybrids of great beauty and distinction. The genus has undoubtedly become one of the most popular of all as regards hybridization, a fact immediately apparent on reference to *Sander's List,* and the hybridization is being carried out most enthusiastically by orchidologists in the countries from which the species come or those with a similar climate. The vast majority of new hybrids have been registered from Malaysia, Hawaii and mainland U.S.A., and many dramatic forms have been evolved.

The genus *Vanda* – the Indian name of the original species – was first described by Robert Brown and is distributed, like *Phalaenopsis,* over most of the Far East. In common with that genus it has also been used very extensively in hybridization. Not only have the species been intercrossed but the genus has been interbred with many other allied genera, including *Arachnis, Aerides, Renenthera, Saccolabium, Vandopsis,* and *Phalaenopsis.*

The genus is mostly epiphytic and has no pseudobulbs, the thick fleshy leaves performing the function of pseudobulbs for storage purposes. There are two main sections, the more attractive having flat or strap-like leaves and the other terete or cylindrical leaves. There are over sixty distinct species, perhaps one of the most famous being *V. coerulea,* from northern India and Burma, for the very striking colour of its flowers. These are a delicate light blue – a colour very rare in the orchid family – with darker tesselations. This species was first discovered by William Griffith in 1837 in the Khasia Hills. It grows at a height of 3,000–5,000 feet, fully exposed to the sun, wind and rain during the flowering period, with summer temperatures of 60–80°F (16–27°C) but much lower in winter, up to ten degrees of frost being usual.

The genus *Dendrobium* – named after the Greek for 'tree' and 'life' – is immense, having upwards of 1,500 species. It is distributed over an equally vast area in South-east Asia, southern India, Japan, New Zealand, Australia, the Malayan Archipelago, the Society Islands and the islands of the Western Pacific. Although all the species necessarily have a close family connection, they are often very different from each other and several attempts have been made to classify them into sections – Lindley, for example, suggested ten, Bentham seven. The species can vary greatly in size, some being so tiny that it is difficult to distinguish them from the moss in which they are found, while others are huge with pseudobulbs four feet in length. Similarly, the vegetative differences – especially of the reproductive organs – are wide; some species have flat leaves, while others have cylindrical stems and leaves. Species such as *D. formosum* grow in hot steamy conditions while others – *D. infundibulum,* for example – are found in cooler moist surroundings. The genus was founded by the Swedish botanist Oloff Swartz in 1800 with a description of nine species.

J Nugent Fitch del et lith

DENDROBIUM SUPERBIENS.

B.S.Williams Publ.

The genus *Dendrobium* is immense, having
more than 1,500 species which are often very
dissimilar in size and shape. The Australian
D. bigibbum was flowered at Kew as early as
1824.

Dendrobium thyrsiflorum, a very different type
of dendrobium from the one opposite, comes
from the forests of Moulmein and Lower
Burma.

The life
of an orchid

In nature almost all orchid flowers, whether terrestrial, epiphytic or lithophytic species, are fertilized by insects. Even in the nineteenth century there was great interest in this aspect of orchidology, both in the Old and the New Worlds. Darwin was fascinated by the subject and published his delightful book, *The Various Contrivances by which Orchids are Fertilised by Insects* in 1862, while in the United States the famous botanist, Asa Gray, mentioned the subject in his *Enumeration of Plants of the Rocky Mountains* (American Journal of Science and Arts, 1862). In the following year J. H. Scudder dealt with it in relation to *Pogonia ophioglossoides*, a species widely distributed in America – to Minnesota in the west and southern Florida in the south, as well as Nova Scotia and Newfoundland. By the time the second edition of Darwin's book was published in 1904, the interest was worldwide and findings had been published by American, Australian, British, German, Italian, New Zealand and South African botanists on the orchids native to their own continents.

Although there are some species which are self-fertilizing, most species, as has already been stated, are fertilized by insects, and during the course of evolution some have developed the most ingenious and varied adaptations to ensure their pollination – and thus their survival.

The *Cattleya* and allied genera, those endowed with a beautiful fringed labellum – often with gold streaking at its throat leading to the column at the apex of which is the pollen – attract large insects such as bees and wasps by means of a sweet perfume as well as the gold 'honey guides'. The labellum, depressed by the bee on landing to allow it to pass down to the nectary, springs back into place and the bee finds itself trapped. In its struggle to escape the bee presses against the pollinia – in the *Cattleya* genus these are usually four in number and attached to the column by sticky, elastic, thready stems – which become fastened to its back. On its next visit to a flower the pollinia brush off and adhere to the stigmatic surface of the column, which is also tacky, and in this way the flower is fertilized. The pollinia are disc-shaped and each contains thousands of pollen grains.

In the *Paphiopedilum* genus the insect becomes trapped in the boat- or shoe-shaped pouch and can escape only by passing through one of two narrow exit gaps or tunnels in which the pollinia are placed in the exact position for easy removal.

Odontoglossum, Miltonia, Oncidum and other kindred genera are usually fertilized by butterflies or moths, which the flowers mimic in shape, size and colour. The moth, mistaking the flower for another moth, carries on a vigorous courtship which in its result is rewarding only to the orchid. *Oncidium papilio* and *O. kramerianum* in particular resemble huge brilliantly coloured butterflies, an impression enhanced by the hovering motion imparted to the long-stemmed flowers by the gentlest breeze. This method of attracting a pollinizing agent by insect mimicry is also adopted by some species of the Mediterranean genus *Ophrys,* which not only look like female wasps but also emit the same odour as a female ready for mating.

Angraecum sesquipedale, the white Christmas Star orchid from Madagascar, has a twelve-inch spur-like nectary below the labellum in which the nectar is gathered right in the tip. Darwin reasoned that only an insect which could reach the nectar could pollinate the flower and therefore postulated the existence of

Although, from a breeder's viewpoint, this flower shows all the deficiencies of a poor paphiopedilum hybrid—narrow petals and waisted dorsal sepal—it displays clearly the disc and one of the pollinia on the right.

Pl 189

J. Nugent Fitch del. et lith

CATASETUM MACROCARPUM.

B.S. Williams Publr

'some huge moth, with a wonderfully long proboscis . . . capable of extension to a length of between ten and eleven inches! This belief of mine has been ridiculed by some entomologists . . .' Nevertheless, forty years later Darwin's theory was proved correct by the discovery on the island of a night-flying species of moth with a tongue twelve inches long, *Xanthopan morgani praedicta*.

Certain catasetums are fertilized in perhaps the most dramatic manner of all. The labellum is in the form of a helmet or an upturned cap at the top of the flower and the pollen is held at the end of a member similar to a coiled spring. There is no nectar but the thickened labellum tastes equally good to a bee and as it gnaws through the cap it touches one of two long antennae which are extremely sensitive. This activates the spring-like mechanism causing the pollen to be ejected forcibly—sometimes to a distance of several inches—on to the bee's head or thorax, and in due course this is deposited on the stigma of the next flower visited by the bee.

After pollination, the sepals and petals wilt and shrivel. This condition does not occur to such an obvious extent during the fertilization of paphiopedilums or of cymbidiums, but in the case of cymbidiums, although the sepals and petals remain apparently unchanged, the lip becomes suffused with dark pink very rapidly. This probably accounts for the statement in a newspaper that 'The orchid blushes when it is married'. This is also the reason for an R.H.S. rule that a flower must be entire when it is put before the Orchid Committee.

It is possible to gain an idea of the life cycle of orchids in general by following in detail what happens to a cattleya after it has been fertilized. A day or two after the pollinia have been deposited on the stigma, the pollen forms a glutinous mass with the viscid substance it secretes. The column has a central duct, containing elongated cells, which leads to the ovary at its base and through which the pollen tubes make their way to the ovary. At first the ovary is circular in cross section with three lines radiating from the centre to the circumference. After about fourteen days the walls of the ovary thicken and the lines widen causing the cross-section outline of the ovary to alter from circular to triangular. These lines are the placentas and after a further fortnight the ovary develops rudimentary ovules attached to the placentas and the pollen tubes start to enter the ovary, making their way down the sides of the placentas and between the ovules. At the end of about two months, the pollen tubes fill the ovary and are situated along the placentas and among the ovules which have not yet been fertilized. In three more weeks, however, the ovules start to develop in size and to alter their shape and by the end of five months, when each pollen tube has entered a small orifice in each ovule—the micropyle—to fertilize it, the process is almost complete. In a temperate climate the pod needs still more time in order to ripen, and this depends on the weather, a long, sunny spell causing the ripening to be shorter, and vice versa. In nature, where there are always at least twelve hours of intense sunlight, the process will no doubt be much quicker. In addition, some genera mature the pods more rapidly than cattleyas, and there is also considerable variation among species even within this genus.

At the end of a year—in some species it may be months earlier or in others take as long as fourteen months—the pod starts to dehisce by splitting along the sides, usually beginning at the apex. This is caused by the drying out of the pod and in nature the seed, which is also dry and powdery, is then wind-borne, much falling on 'stony ground' and only a very small percentage finding a resting place where it is able to germinate.

This fertilization routine is followed by the hybridizer, that is, by removing the pollen from the anther and placing it on the stigmatic surface. The pollen tubes pass down the inside of the column in exactly the same way as when the flower is fertilized by an insect in nature, the ovules are entered by the pollen tubes and an embryo formed in each ovule. In a good cattleya seed capsule there can be tens of thousands of fertile seeds.

It is at this point that the similarity of the process of fertilization by insect in the jungle and by man in an orchid house ends, for after about five months, when the fertilization of the cattleya has been completed and each ovule has its embryo, man can do what is impossible in nature and remove the fertile ovules from the placentas by scraping them off in sterile conditions and then inoculating (sowing) flasks with them as described on page 81, thus saving several months of the germination period. It has been found that this method is more successful, if performed skilfully, than if the full period were allowed to elapse.

In nature seed is carried indiscriminately by the wind and only that succeeds which is lucky enough to find the right conditions for germination. Unlike the seeds of most other plants, orchid seeds possess no food store on which to draw while germinating. Instead, every species develops a symbiotic relationship—mutually beneficial partnership—with certain fungi, and because the seed cannot survive alone during its early stages it will perish unless it makes immediate contact with the right type of fungus.

After six months, the seed becomes a tiny speck of green vegetation which, if viewed under a microscope, appears bowl-shaped with a little peak at the top. After a further period of three months, the peak has developed into what is undoubtedly a leaf, and at the end of a year there are two pairs of leaves and several short, white rootlets. In another four months the speck has become a recognizable cattleya plantlet, and from then on makes rapid progress. The roots grow fastest because the life of the plant will depend on how efficiently they anchor the plant to the tree. They do not bring much nourishment to the plant as their main function is to keep the plant attached to its host. The only green showing in the root is about half an inch or so at the tip (the growing part), the rest of the root being covered with a fleshy white 'sleeve', absorbent to a certain degree but otherwise incapable of taking in nourishment for the plant.

The cattleya plant in the jungle grows more rapidly than its glasshouse counterpart if only because in its natural habitat it is subjected to much longer periods of light of a much higher average daily intensity. All green plants depend for life on the action of light on their green parts, that is, their leaves and, in the case of the cattleya, the green tips of its roots. If, in addition to the longer hours of light, there is an added bonus of extra warmth—especially during the day—this action is hastened; carbon dioxide is taken in more rapidly during the hours of day-

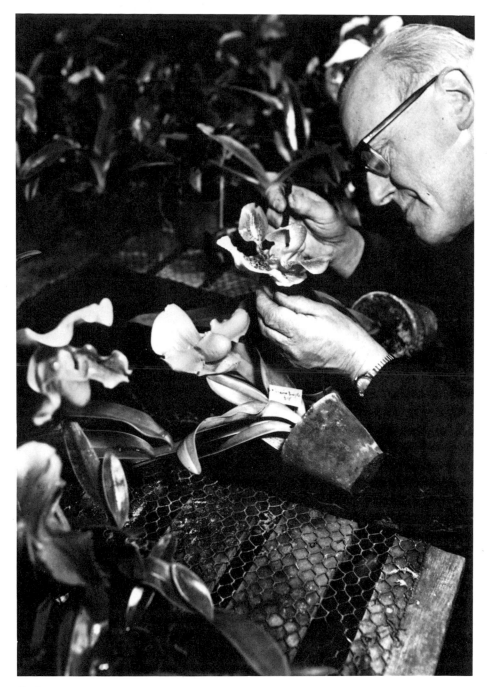

The author is removing the pollen mass or pollina from the right-hand side of the labellum of a *Paphiopedilum* hybrid.

light and converted into sugar during the hours of darkness, the plant's cells multiply more rapidly and the plant therefore grows more vigorously and quickly. The advantage of glasshouse growing is that all the preceding plant activities can be observed and noted, whereas it is well-nigh impossible to do this in the jungle.

The cattleya life cycle described above is similar to that of many other orchids and nearly all epiphytes, although the way the capsule dehisces is different in many genera. Some split in three places from top to bottom, some have two valves, some three, while others remain attached to each other at the apex or at the base; one at least splits into three separate sections, each having the seed attached to the median line – or mid-rib – running from apex to base.

The amount of seed in most capsules varies, but is usually immense in quantity. Darwin calculated that if every one of the approximately 6,200 seeds produced by the average thirty capsules of the small European Spotted Orchid (*Orchis maculata*)

germinated successfully it could cover the entire land surface of the earth in three generations. Some tropical species reveal an even greater abundance; 3,700,000 seeds were found by scientific count in a single pod of the Venezuelan *Cynoches chlorochilon*. Why does nature provide such bountiful numbers? The proportion of orchid flowers actually pollinated in the wild is very tiny and the amount of seed finding a congenial resting place and the right fungus to enable it to germinate is minute. Again only the most vigorous survive. When sown in laboratory conditions, however, most of the seed germinates and is duly pricked off and cultivated. The vigorous, the less vigorous and the downright unwilling are all grown, but some are quick to reach maturity and some slow. This is reflected in the time taken to reach flowering size and to produce flowers. In the *Paphiopedilum* genus, for example, a hybrid will flower in four and a half years from the date of sowing, but out of the same batch some will not flower for perhaps a further five years. It is, however, these slow-growing varieties which are often the best.

The tropical Butterfly Orchid is native to many parts of South America. Its brilliant, apparently hovering flowers mimic the gorgeously coloured butterflies which are deceived into thinking them potential mates and thus bring about pollination.

The Mirror Orchid—so-called because of the glossy, mirror-like, blue spot on the disc—is a member of the genus *Ophrys* to which many of the European mimics of insects belong

The orchid collectors

Towards the end of the first quarter of the nineteenth century the great horticultural firms started to send collectors to the remote jungles of the world in search of new tropical plants and seeds of trees. Often items quite apart from those of horticultural interest were also collected on these expeditions—Richard Pearce, for instance, set off hopefully on a hunt for 'plants, seeds, land-shells and other objects of natural history'. Rollisons of Tooting were among the first to import orchid plants in any significant number but their importations appeared a mere trickle in comparison to the flood of plants brought into the country in the 1890s and early 1900s when importations of 30,000 orchids of a single species became commonplace. These plants were sold at auction within hours of their arrival—often amidst scenes of great excitement—first at Stevens's Auction Rooms and later in the auction hall of Protheroe and Morris.

The orchid hunters who risked their lives to collect these plants were truly heroic, even by Victorian standards. Motivated by an almost obsessive love of the plants they were collecting and —in most cases—by an unshakeable loyalty to their employers, the histories of their adventures read like stories from the *Boy's Own Paper*; the constant battle of wits between rival collectors, the treasons and stratagems they employed to outmanoeuvre each other would have done justice to present-day industrial espionage. But their world—the whole way of life of which orchids had been such a typical expression—came to an abrupt end on the outbreak of the First World War in 1914 and even prior to this there were signs of change. The despoiling of the world's tropical wild places could not continue unchecked and the trade in the export of tropical species never recovered.

Although dried specimens of orchid plants had frequently been sent home to botanists, it was not until the early part of the eighteenth century that a tropical orchid first flowered in England. In 1731 a dried herbarium specimen of *Bletia verecunda*

The expedition which E. André led up the
River Caura, a tributary of the Orinoco in
Venezuela, in the first year of this century
must have been very similar to some of the
orchid-hunting expeditions undertaken a
little earlier. The top picture shows
Waiomgomos, the local tribesmen, bringing in
plants of *Cattleya superba* and (below) the
arrival of a boatload of orchids at La Prision.

Far left: Typical Panamanian jungle, showing the kind of terrain traversed by orchid hunters

Bringing home a fine clump of *Cattleya* species on a more recent collecting expedition in Guyana

The leaves of several epiphytic and lithophytic species of orchid can be seen in this Venezuelan jungle scene

was sent to Peter Collinson from Providence Island in the Bahamas. 'But the tuber appearing to have life in it' he potted it and gave it to a Mr Wager who succeeded in producing a bloom. After this attempts were made to cultivate several different types of orchid but without much success as faulty information was given by the collectors about the habitat from which they came and the hothouses in which they were grown, heated by underground flues using solid fuel, were quite unsuitable for their culture.

Dr John Fothergill brought two orchids home with him on his return from China, one of which, *Phaius grandifolius,* flowered in his niece's Yorkshire hothouse and in 1787–8, about ten years later, two more orchids, *Epidendrum cochleatum* and *E. fragrans* from South America, flowered in the Royal Botanic Gardens at Kew. By the time the first edition of Alton's *Hortus Kewensis* appeared in 1789 the author was able to state that fifteen exotic species were in cultivation there.

With the founding of the Horticultural Society in 1809 horticulture generally and orchids in particular were given vast encouragement; they ceased to be looked on as mere curiosities and were cultivated seriously. It seems, however, that whether from the hot steamy river valleys of South America or the cool slopes of the Andes and the Mexican highlands, all orchids were given the same treatment; on arrival they were consigned to the 'stove' (the hottest house) and plunged into pots containing a mixture of decayed leaves which were then half buried in a tan-pit. Nevertheless, Sir Joseph Banks was successful in growing orchids at his house near Richmond, Surrey, from 1815–20.

During the years 1824–27 the Curator of the Botanical Gardens in Trinidad sent many orchids to Kew with detailed instructions for their cultivation, which naturally ensured a much longer life for the plants. At about the same time the Horticultural Society began experimenting, under the direction of Dr Lindley, to discover the best method of growing orchids. The results of this research were published in 1830 but were, unfortunately, rather misleading since no mention was made of ventilation and the different needs of different types of orchid depending on their natural habitat. Collectors who realized the importance of describing thoroughly the type of conditions in which a newly discovered species was growing all stressed the fact that the orchids they collected were growing in cool conditions and could not be expected to thrive when given the treatment in current use. It is doubtful whether their instructions were always followed and it was left to the example of practical gardeners who understood the value of ventilation and temperature control to be seen and copied.

The most remarkable of these practical gardeners was Joseph Paxton who was in charge of the Duke of Devonshire's gardens at Chatsworth. The orchid collection there was started in 1833 and was constantly improved and increased by the acquisition of good varieties and by importations of rare species. Indeed, the Duke was so enthusiastic that he sent out his own collector, Gibson, to the Khasia Hills. After he had travelled up the Brahmaputra into Assam Gibson reported back that he had already collected fifty different species 'some of them beautiful beyond description or comparison'. Many of the considerable

Dendrobium gibsonii, one of the species discovered in the Khasia Hills in 1836 by the Duke of Devonshire's collector, Gibson, and named after him

numbers of species he sent home were previously quite unknown to European gardeners. Paxton had always been willing to divulge his methods for the benefit of other less well situated growers, and in 1834 he started the publication of the *Magazine of Botany* in which he detailed the progress towards the rationalization of the cultivation of different genera of orchids for which he became so renowned. After fifteen years its name was changed to *Paxton's Flower Garden*; John Lindley became the editor and continued its policy of including cultural and other notes about orchids.

The commercial establishments, too, were in the forefront of the struggle to better cultivation and from Backhouse of York to Veitch, Loddiges, Rollisons and Low, experiments were carried out and new methods evolved. It was at about this period that the commercial establishments started to send out collectors in earnest.

Typical of the times is the history of some of Veitch's travellers. In 1840, when Veitch had not yet taken over the Chelsea establishment, he sent William Lobb, a young Cornishman who had been employed at the Exeter Nursery, on a collecting expedition to South America; he landed at Rio de Janeiro and discovered several fine orchid species of an extreme rarity in England, thus becoming the first commercial orchid hunter. One of his most striking introductions was *Cypripedium* (now transferred to *Phragmipedium*) *caudatum* from Peru. This has large flowers with long red-brown, ribbon-like petals nearly three feet in length, yellowish-green at their base, and a creamy-yellow dorsal sepal tinged and veined with green.

Three years later his brother Thomas also set out as a collector and proved to be by far the most successful of Veitch's plant hunters, probably because his contract gave him a great deal of discretion about where he should collect. He set off for the Far East and, finding that China was far from interested in having a European botanical collector operating in her territory, he visited Java and the adjacent islands. On his second tour he was sent to India for three years and arrived in Calcutta on Christmas Day, 1848. He was with Veitch for twenty years and during that time he collected a great number of seeds and plants of various kinds, including over thirty different species of orchid—many introduced to cultivation for the first time. Among these are species which are now household names to orchidists, such as *Vanda coerulea*, first discovered by W. Griffiths in 1837 and one of the very rare blue members of the orchid family, and *Paphiopedilum villosum*, a glossy orange-red tinged with green and purple. Although he spent some time in the various orchid-hunting grounds of north-eastern India, such as Assam and the Khasia Hills, he also collected many fine orchids in Burma. He then visited the southern Malayan Archipelago, Labuan and Sarawak, afterwards travelling on to the Philippines where he collected in the area around Manila. In spite of all his travels—and there were undoubted hardships and dangers undergone by all travellers at that time—he survived until 1894, enjoying a peaceful retirement in his native Cornwall.

Old age was rare among plant collectors, however. *Hortus Veitchii* records how in one two-year period three of the firm's collectors died young, their health broken by tropical disease and

Dendrobium densiflorum, one of the many
dendrobiums found on the lower slopes of
the Himalayas

Cattleya mossiae reineckiana belongs to the labiata group of cattleyas and is native to the jungles of Venezuela

Below: This picture of *Dendrobium aphyllum* illustrates the undoubtedly epiphytic habit of its genus. Epiphytic species created many problems for their collectors.

the severity of the conditions in which they worked, while yet another lost his life by drowning. Often, too, these tragic deaths seem to have resulted from a mere whim of fate. For example, David Bowman, having collected a large number of plants near Bogota, suffered a heavy loss through robbery almost on the eve of his departure for England and was obliged to stay; he contracted dysentry during this period of enforced waiting and died shortly after. Even Veitch's own son, John Gould, who was particularly successful in collecting various species of *Phalaenopsis* in the Philippines, died from a lung infection when he was only thirty-one.

Sometimes collectors came to plant hunting from circles quite outside horticulture; J. Henry Chesterton's niche in life before he became interested in orchids was that of gentleman's gentleman. After being coached at Veitch's Chelsea nursery in the art of packing plants for long journeys he disappeared from the London scene for a while and then turned up with 'a collection of orchids so well packed and well looked after, that they arrived in the best possible condition'. After this he made several journeys to South America and succeeded, where other and more experienced collectors had failed, in collecting and introducing to England the long-sought, so-called 'scarlet Odontoglossum', which is now known as *Miltonia vexillaria*.

One of the strangest and most successful of Veitch's travellers was Gustave Wallis. Born deaf and dumb and unable to articulate until he was six years old, he yet became fluent in foreign languages. He was apprenticed to a gardener at Detmold in Germany and eventually went to Brazil to start a branch of a German horticultural firm. When this firm failed in 1858 he was more or less stranded and offered to collect plants for Linden of Brussels, during his search exploring the Amazon together with some of its larger tributaries from mouth to source. He joined Veitch in 1870 and sent home many fine plants from New Grenada, including the scented *Epidendrum wallisii*. This orchid is remarkable for the size of its golden-yellow, crimson-spotted flowers and the continuity with which they are produced.

There were not only professional collectors, subsidized by the large firms, but also unpaid and enthusiastic expatriates whose duties took them to the orchid-growing countries or who had businesses in them. Among these were Colonel Benson, who sent Veitch many new and rare species from Burma, Sir Hugh Low, the Colonial Secretary in Labuan, North Borneo, who discovered many of the then unknown orchids in that orchid paradise, and Mr G. Ure-Skinner who sent home to Veitch and to the Horticultural Society innumerable species from Guatemala. Bateman, the author of *Orchidaceae of Mexico and Guatemala*, wrote to Mr Skinner craving his assistance and received an unexpectedly favourable reply. 'From the moment he received our letter he has laboured almost incessantly to drag from their hiding places the forest treasures of Guatemala, and transfer them to the stoves of his native land. In pursuit of this object there is scarcely a sacrifice which he has not made, or a danger or hardship he has not braved . . . he may truly be said to have been the means of introducing a greater number of new and beautiful Orchidaceae into Europe than any one individual of his own or any other nation'. There are several Guatemalan species named after him.

Dendrobium lituiflorum is a spring-flowering species which is widely distributed over northern India, Burma and Thailand.

Louis Forget on his way through a village in Colombia with a consignment of cattleyas collected for Sander.

During the late 1870s the name of Frederick Sander begins to appear more and more frequently and by the end of the century the House of Sander had come to dominate the orchid-hunting world. He employed at one time and another nearly a score of collectors, the best and most likeable of whom were Arnold, Forget and Micholitz, and often had many men collecting simultaneously—sometimes in the same part of the world—so that there was competition not only between his firm and his business rivals but between his own collectors. His most bitter battles were waged against Low, whose chief collector was Boxall, and against the Belgian firm Linden, for whom Claes and Bungeroth were the principal plant hunters. He took an intense personal interest in the progress of his collectors, writing frequent letters of instruction and admonition which included any details he had managed to glean of rival collectors' movements, for it had become a common practise for one orchid hunter to spend days or even weeks tracking another if it was suspected that he was 'on to something good' and much ingenuity was employed in spying and leaving false trails and information. In one letter Sander, much upset by a rather underhand business stratagem employed by Low to outwit him, writes to Arnold, 'up to now I've been able to bear Low, since he is someone with whom a fight is worthwhile, . . . even if one has a show-down . . . But since the fellow has behaved so loutishly we must do all we can to get even. I hope that before you get these lines you will be on the way to Merida and get there ahead of White (Low's collector). Just do the fellow down.' And in another letter to Arnold he

warns that he has just heard that a devil called Burke from
Veitch's is right behind him.

One of Sander's greatest triumphs was the introduction in
1881 of the vanda named after him, *Vanda sanderiana*. It was
described by Reichenbach in the *Gardener's Chronicle* as, 'The
grandest novelty introduced for years – a golden letter day. . .
From the top of the odd sepal to the top of the lateral ones, the
flower measure(s) five inches . . . the odd sepals and petals are
mauve with some basilar purple stripes; the lateral sepals are
yellow, washed with brown and with broad purple veins; the
border is mauve and lip dark brown, with green sides. The
column is golden yellow. Some plants bore five peduncle(s) at
one time. One had three spikes with forty-seven flowers and
buds, thirty-four being open at one time, thus presenting the
appearance of a giant bouquet.' It was first collected by Carl
Roebelin on Mindanao in the Philippines in the most dramatic
circumstances, as Arthur Swinson relates in *The Orchid King*.

On arrival at the island Roebelin heard rumours of a beautiful
red orchid growing on the north coast of the island which from
its description appeared to be a species of *Phalaenopsis*. He
abandoned his unsuccessful search on the coast, however, on
being told of an orchid 'with flowers the size of dinner plates'
growing on the shores of a lake in the interior. With the help of a
Chinese trader as interpreter and guide he made his way up
river by sampan to the lake, only to be shipwrecked in a sudden
squall of hurricane-force wind which whipped the water into
giant waves. He was rescued by tribesmen who were, luckily,
well-disposed towards Europeans because they wanted support in
their wars against a neighbouring tribe. Proof of this was soon
given as the war trumpets of hostile tribesmen were heard
approaching the village. Fortunately the outcome of the battle
was successful for the tribesmen with whom he was encamped
and Roebelin was alotted a place for the night in the chief's tree-
house high above the ground. In the words of Frederick Boyle,
'It was a roar and a rush like the crack of doom which woke him;
shrieking and shouting, clang of things which fell, boom of great
waves, and thunder such as mortal never heard dominating all'.
Clinging to the heaving and tossing floor, with bodies flying past
him and crashing through the walls of the hut into the surround-
ing blackness, Roebelin was at the centre of the worst earthquake
the Philippines had ever known. When the tremors had ceased
and day finally dawned he found himself still on the floor of the
shattered hut with the walls in shreds about him; through one of
the great holes in the floor he saw a spray not of the scarlet
Phalaenopsis he was seeking but of one of the most beautiful
orchids he had ever seen, a glory of mauve, purple, gold and
brown: *Vanda sanderiana* had been discovered.

Similar stories could be told about the discovery of many
species and always the collectors show an equal courage and
intrepidity. Forsterman, another of Sander's orchid hunters,
spent months in Assam in pursuit of *Cypripedium spicerianum*, an
unknown orchid which had first flowered in the collection of a
lady living in Wimbledon and created a sensation in the London
salerooms. His search led him to jungles which were so dense
that the only means of making progress was to wade up the icy
mountain streams traversing them. Just as he was about to give

A drawing of *Oncidium cavendishianum* made
in the field by Forget and sent home to
Frederick Sander in a letter

up he finally came upon large numbers of the orchid growing at the top of a sheer rocky outcrop. Even then his troubles were not at an end; he had to kill a tiger which was ravaging the village from which his Bhutani porters came before they would agree to transport the orchids to the Brahmaputra so that he could get them to a port. He was successful for eventually Sander offered 40,000 *Cypripedium spicerianum* for sale on one day alone at Stevens's Auction Rooms.

When an area of the jungle was discovered in which a single species of orchid was growing in thousands – and if this species was one which would be saleable at home – the collector would strip the area as completely as he could, not so much to enhance his own profits as to deny others the chance. The plants were

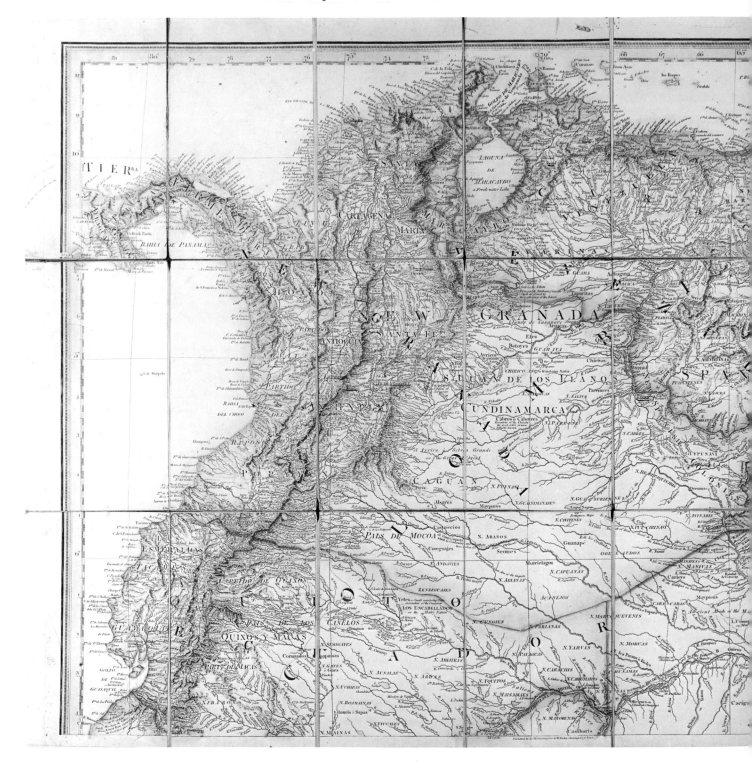

then transported, sometimes hundreds of miles, to the nearest port, there to be packed and shipped home for delivery to the auction rooms in London.

Frequently the timing of the arrival of the plants at the port was bad and they remained slowly rotting in the sun as they waited for a ship, or whole consignments were lost at sea—or even before they were put aboard ship, as Roebelin, who had at last succeeded in finding the scarlet *Phalaenopsis,* reported to Sander from Manila, 'A shameful misfortune has overcome me—destroyed in a few minutes all the plants I had! The lot! In the frightful hurricane . . . everything went west. . . . Not until the third day was it possible to see the plants, and they were beaten down to the ground and the huts were flooded with mud and

Below left: Map used in the field by Louis Forget, who was in command of all Sander's collectors in South America; it is marked with crosses denoting the areas in which orchids had been found.

The type of terrain the collectors often had to traverse in their search for new orchid species.

This advertisement appeared in *The Gardeners' Chronicle* for September 26th, 1891. *Cattleya labiata* was first discovered in the Orgao Mountains north of Rio de Janeiro by Mr William Swainson in 1818. Sander's excitement is understandable as the orchid had been 'lost' for over sixty years.

salt-water. In spite of instant washing in fresh water not one of the 21,000 specimens remains. All the other orchids were lost too. All I had.' So Roebelin returned to collect some more.

And Micholitz, having finally rediscovered the 'lost' *Dendrobium phalaenopsis schroederianum*, saw his entire cargo—worth thousands of pounds in London—go up in flames when the ship on which it was loaded caught fire in the port of Macassar on Celebes. The exchange of telegrams which resulted reveals much of Sander's indomitable will. As reported by Swinson, Micholitz cabled, 'SHIP BURNT WHAT DO MICHOLITZ', which evoked the response, 'RETURN RECOLLECT'. Micholitz replied 'TOO LATE – RAINY SEASON', but Sander was unshakeable, back came the reply, 'RETURN SANDER', and the dendrobiums were put up for auction on 16th October, 1891.

The auction rooms, or halls, in London acted as clearing houses where the tens of thousands of orchid plants were quickly and efficiently distributed among the eager orchid fanciers of the time. At first J. C. Stevens's Auction Rooms handled the great bulk of orchid importations but after Sander had had a dispute with Stevens most of this business was eventually taken over by Protheroe and Morris. They handled thousands of orchid species during the heyday of importations and carried on by offering hybrids for auction after the decline in popularity of species. Their auction premises were, unfortunately for the orchid industry, destroyed during the Second World War by a direct hit; however the firm, now Protheroe, Reynolds and Easton, still continues with the auction of orchids, but either on the grower's nursery or in convenient halls elsewhere.

The excitement generated by the news of the forthcoming sale of a hitherto rare or new species – *Vanda sanderiana,* for example – was immense, and the rooms were crowded long before the auction was due to start. The spectacle of hundreds of top-hatted orchidophiles arriving by hansom cab or brougham and milling around trying to assess the value of individual plants, the gradual ceasing of chatter while one of the Morrises mounted the rostrum to begin the proceedings in complete silence, must have been an impressive experience.

The numbers of orchid plants which were collected and lost, or offered at auction – for example, the 40,000 *Cypripedium spicerianum* already mentioned – seem stupendous to modern minds, and also senseless, for the law of diminishing returns inevitably came into play.

With the advent of the Great War in 1914 came the end of orchid collecting on the grand scale. It had been declining, for several reasons, since 1900: the jungles had been so efficiently combed for new plants that there seemed little new of worth to discover; hybridization had increased and hybrids were more popular with their greater variety of colour, shape and size; and also the 'big spenders' were not operating to anything like the same degree. The war years saw the finish of many private orchid houses and the commercial firms had taken a battering from which the recovery was long and painful; both private collections and commercial establishments were re-built mostly by hybrids of the popular genera. The species – of which there were a mere trickle compared with the flood of the last part of the nineteenth century – were collected by people who had either settled in the orchid countries or who were native-born and started nurseries, collecting and exporting plants from the jungle as a useful side-line. At rather too late a stage in the proceedings, the governments of these countries woke up to the fact that their environment had been harmed, and imposed restrictions on the collection and export of live plants. The Golden Age of Orchids in England was apparently over.

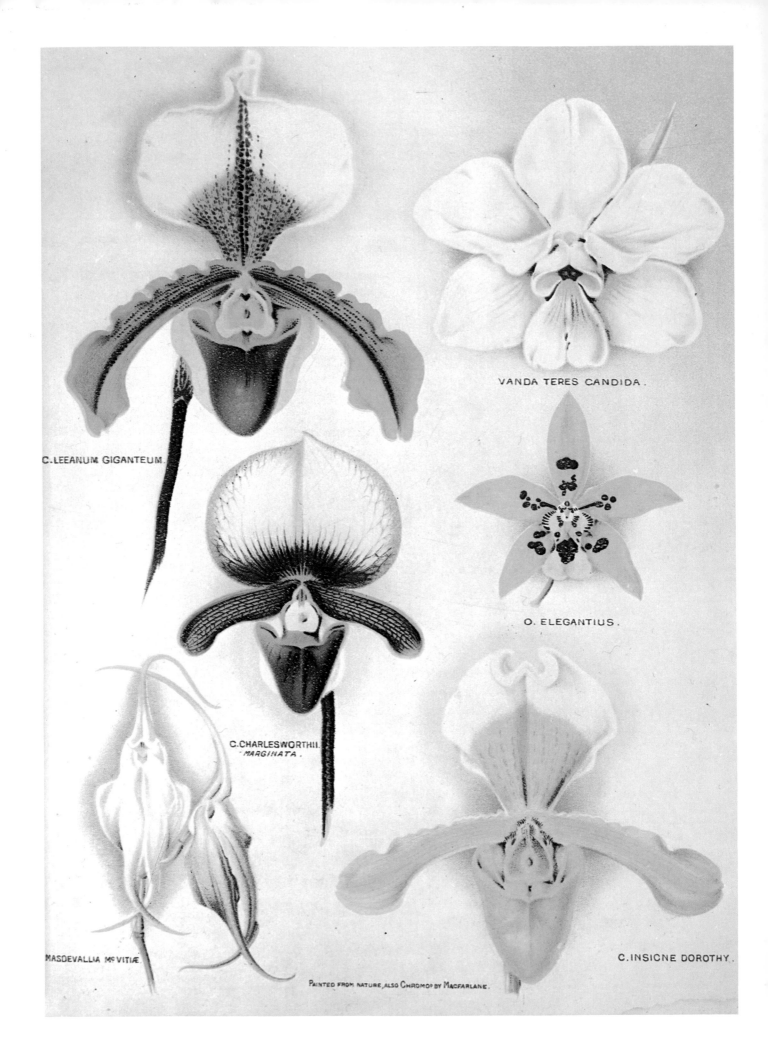

VANDA TERES CANDIDA.

C.LEEANUM GIGANTEUM.

O. ELEGANTIUS.

C.CHARLESWORTHII.
MARGINATA.

MASDEVALLIA Mc VITIÆ.

C.INSIGNE DOROTHY.

Painted from nature, also Chromo? by Macfarlane.

SOPHRONITIS GRANDIFLORA.

Left: A page from a sale catalogue of Protheroe and Morris dated 1898. The orchids being sold belonged to William Thompson who owned one of the finest collections in the country at that time.

Sophronitis grandiflora, a native of the jungles of Brazil, is in the pedigree of most of the sophrocattleyas, sophrolaeliocattleyas and potinaras of today.

The propagation of orchids

It is easy to be wise after the event but it is, nevertheless, a little puzzling to understand why it took so long to hybridize orchids since, by the time John Dominy flowered the now famous cross between two calanthes in 1856, taxonomists had been studying the reproductive organs of the flower for more than 100 years. As early as 1793 Sprengel observed that insects were necessary for orchid pollination and this fact was again pointed out by Robert Brown. Despite Dominy's success there was an almost unanimous disbelief among botanists and even those whose judgement was not impaired by prejudice were affronted by the unnaturalness of the hybrid and stigmatized it as a 'mule' incapable of reproduction by fertilization. It took the great John Lindley more than a year before he could bring himself to describe the progeny of the cross.

Although this general attitude was greatly modified by the publication of Darwin's work on the fertilization of orchids, it was probably largely responsible – together with the almost obsessive interest of many collectors in the vast quantities of new species flooding the market during the latter half of the nineteenth century – for the long delay in developing hybridization. It was not until sixteen years after Dominy's initial success that his first emulator appeared; Lady Ashburton and her grower Mr Cross flowered *Cypripedium* (now *Paphiopedilum*) *barbatum* × *C. insigne* and named it *C. Ashburtoniae*. This was the first of well over 150 crosses to be made with *insigne* as one parent, and it is still in the pedigree of most, if not all, modern hybrids. It was thirty-one years before there was any challenge from a trade competitor. Although Veitch no longer had the field to them-

Tiny orchid plants growing in 'flats'. The white labels refer to the stud book numbers.

selves they had had a handsome start and by the time Seden, who followed Dominy and was trained by him, retired in 1905 he had raised over 500 hybrids.

This number raised over so many years seems unimpressive when hybrids are now churned out in the abundance with which species used to be imported, but the present torrent of hybrids owes its generation and proliferation to a sequence of events which have revolutionized orchid culture.

In 1885 a German botanist, A. B. Frank, discovered that wild orchid seed germinates with the help of a fungus with which it is infected and coined the word 'mycorrhiza' to describe the association. The relationship between two organisms of different kinds which contribute to each other's support is called symbiosis. Initially the fungus provides sufficient nourishment to enable the orchid seed to germinate – unlike the seeds of most other plants it has no food store on which to draw – and later feeds on nutrients produced by the germinating seed.

Paphiopedilum Blackburn var. November, a handsome modern hybrid. Research is at present being carried out into the possibility of reproducing paphiopedilums by a method similar to the meristem.

Left: The author in his laboratory examining a flask of cattleya plants ready to be pricked off to a community pot

Top right: Sophrolaeliocattleya 'Salamander', the result of crossing between *Cattleya* and its allied genera *Laelia* and *Sophronitis*

Bottom right: Corner of a cymbidium house in southern California. The majority of cymbidiums are grown in the open air in this favoured part of the world and cooling has to be employed in a glass house.

A little later, Noel Bernard, a French scientist who was experimenting with various fungi, succeeded in identifying, isolating and culturing several different species and in 1905 published *Action des microorganismes sur la germination des orchidées*. At about the same time Hans Burgeff was working along the same lines in Germany and also published his findings. Both scientists experimented by sowing different types of orchid seed in various fungal cultures, and Burgeff eventually succeeded in germinating the seed of several different genera by using this symbiotic method. It has not been adopted to any great extent by growers, however, as it requires a certain amount of laboratory technique together with access to a laboratory, and the process of isolating and culturing a particular fungus is not easy except to a scientist.

Before this the method of sowing seed was uncomplicated and, compared with the present system, relatively inefficient, for whereas the old-timers managed to scrape a few hundred seedlings from a pod containing perhaps 500,000 potential plants, the modern grower can in some cases achieve ninety per cent success. The seed was sown on the surface of moistened, sterilized canvas or tiffany stretched over a flower pot containing tightly packed sphagnum moss and kept at a temperature of 75–80°F (24–27°C). The seed was not sterilized nor was any aid to germination such as a nutrient solution or fertilizer used; varying degrees of success were attained depending on the viability of the seed. Another and more certain method of obtaining seedlings was to select a vigorous plant, well established for perhaps a year, and sow the seed on the surface of the compost in which it was growing. Because of the fungus present in most healthy adult plants symbiosis was achieved without the bother of having to isolate the correct fungus. This second method was in some ways easier and achieved better results than the first, but the hazard was in the watering, for if a coarse rose was used on just one occasion the seed could be washed down into the compost and never seen again.

These were the standard methods in use until 1922 when Lewis Knudson, an American scientist, made a discovery which was to have almost as much influence on the raising of hybrids as the production of John Dominy's first hybrid bloom in 1856; this was the asymbiotic method of germinating orchid seed without using a fungus. After exhaustive experiments Professor Knudson found that it could be by-passed by the relatively simple procedure of sowing sterilized seed on a sterilized nutrient in a test-tube, flask or bottle in sterile conditions.

There are now dozens of 'recipes' for the preparation of nutrient solutions but their main components are exactly calculated weights of the various salts necessary for the germination of the seed, certain kinds of sugar such as glucose or laevulose—which comprise by far the largest part of the solution— a quantity of agar-agar (a jelly derived from various seaweeds) in powder, granulated or shredded form, mixed together with distilled water and heated until all the ingredients have dissolved. This mixture is then measured into flasks and sterilized in an autoclave (a laboratory pressure-cooker) for a specified period, usually fifteen minutes at a pressure of fifteen pounds. After cooling a little the flasks are removed and, according to the

Orchid seedlings growing on nutrient solution—an agar slope—in a flask

method being followed, either laid on their sides or left standing upright, for the nutrient to solidify into a firm jelly, the 'agar slope'.

The seed, which is so fine that it looks like a coarse powder unless viewed under a microscope, is then itself sterilized. This is done by placing a quantity—a mere pinch will provide a potential thousand seedlings—into a small phial with a sterilizing fluid such as a solution of calcium hypochlorite (the bleaching powder once used by our grannies) and water; the phial should be shaken and left for fifteen minutes exactly. It was once thought that a period of less than fifteen minutes would not sterilize the outside of the seed thoroughly enough and that contamination in the flask would occur later owing to the sugary nature of the solution, and that a period exceeding fifteen minutes would kill the embryo in the seed. It has recently been proved that in the majority of cases the seed is efficiently sterilized in much less than fifteen minutes.

At the end of the period of sterilization, the seed is sown in the flasks or—to use the technical terminology—the flasks are 'inoculated' as follows: a thin platinum wire in the form of a loop fitted into the end of a short glass rod is passed through the flame of a bunsen burner or spirit lamp and a tiny blob of seed picked up on the platinum loop. The bung is then removed from a flask, the seed quickly distributed over the surface of the agar slope, and the bung and the neck of the flask both sterilized before the bung is firmly inserted into the neck of the flask which is further protected by a square of aluminium foil drawn round it. The flask is then placed back in position and kept at a temperature of 70–75°F (21–24°C). If the flask has been left upright the seed is inoculated through a hole in the rubber bung with a coarse hypodermic syringe.

The simplicity of the asymbiotic method together with its certainty of success in producing seedlings—if correctly followed—transformed orchid culture, but was a mixed blessing as far as orchid hybridization was concerned. Its very simplicity encouraged many amateurs to make the attempt and having once overcome their initial difficulties, due mostly to insufficient care in the sterilizing or clumsy balancing of the ingredients of the nutrient solution, many acquired the correct technique and succeeded in germinating their own seed. A good many of the crosses made were relatively worthless but because the seed had germinated the seedlings were raised to maturity, only for their grower to discover—after a number of years of patient care—that he had been cherishing orchid weeds. This accounts to a large extent for the enormous number of poor hybrids and, sadly, many of them are the direct result of genuine curiosity and enthusiasm.

At the present time a second outstanding development has revolutionized orchid culture even further. It is a method of propagating orchids by means of the apical meristem, that is, the dividing cells at the tip of a growing shoot. This means of propagation was discovered by Georges Morel, a French plant physiologist, during his research to produce a virus-free potato. He found that the apical meristem was clean and had no symptoms of virus. By dissecting tissue from it which he grew in a culture medium he was eventually successful in propagating a virus-free potato. An enthusiastic amateur orchid grower, he applied the same method to cymbidiums in his collection with equal success. His work in this field was taken up by Michel Vacherot and Maurice Lecoufle, commercial orchid growers, who experimented on other genera and obtained sensational results.

At present only those orchids which have pseudobulbs can be treated, but work is being carried out on the *Paphiopedilum* genus, among others, members of which do not have bulbs but make new growths each year. The great importance of this method, however, is in reproducing hybrids which are perfect replicas of the original. Prior to this discovery such replicas could only be reproduced by division of the old plant, a slow process producing, necessarily, only a limited number of plants. By the meristem process the number of copies obtainable is infinite, each identical to the parent plant and to all the others.

The young bud, or the start of what eventually will be a pseudobulb, is removed from the plant of, say, a cymbidium or a cattleya. It is placed on the dissecting stage of a binocular microscope, and the leaves are carefully peeled off until the last pair only is left. These are so small that they look like pinheads. Each piece is divided into four morsels and these are sterilized and put into a flask of nutrient solution, which is then placed in a flask-shaker to agitate the liquid. If examined at the end of a period of about a month, it will be seen that each of the four pieces of plant tissue has developed what appear to be small bumps, but which in reality are the result of the cells multiplying. Each 'mericlone' is again divided and the whole process repeated until the grower has as many mericlones as he needs. From the time the tiny plantlets are removed from the flask they are treated in the same manner as seedlings from inoculated flasks but they grow a little more rapidly. If the process has been carefully followed and proper precautions taken against contamination, the plantlets will be free from any virus which might have been present in the plant from which the original bud was taken.

Inoculated flasks of seed should be kept in the dark for a week or two and then placed in a subdued light. When the seed is especially vigorous—and seed varies greatly—germination can be seen in a week to ten days. The flasks containing meristem propagations can be put in subdued light straight away and from then on both types of seedlings are treated in exactly the same way. As early as six weeks after inoculation the seedlings are large enough to be recognized as such, with tiny leaves and perhaps a root, and at this stage they may either be left to develop further in the original flask or carefully transplanted on to the agar surface of another sterile flask. This is termed 're-plating' and has much to recommend it because the plants grow more quickly and are soon large enough to be pricked off into a community pot, twenty-five to thirty to a pot.

Several years ago the classic potting compost for most genera was osmunda fibre and live sphagnum moss; finely chopped and screened for seedlings and of various grades of coarseness for adult plants. Osmunda fibre became increasingly expensive, however, and 'economy composts' are now in favour. These can include fir bark, sedge peat, sphagnum moss peat, live sphagnum moss, charcoal, polystyrene and other types of plastic, vermiculite or pearlite. Not only are these composts much cheaper but they are readily available, and the process of potting and repotting with this type of material is much easier and very much quicker. The potting skill, so vital when using osmunda fibre, is no longer necessary and this is all part of the process of making orchids easier and easier to grow.

The plantlets are transferred from the community pot after about six months to another pot of the same size but in which only four to five seedlings are planted. A year or so later, the seedlings graduate to a pot each, and from then on to a larger pot each year until they attain maximum size. Often they flower before reaching maximum size; this is especially true of miltonias and odontoglossums. The term 'seedling' can be used to describe both an enormous plant which has not yet flowered, or a wee speck of vegetation, hardly discernible as a plant.

The time taken for the new plant to flower varies according to the genus involved. Paphiopedilums, for example, which are probably the fastest of the 'commercial' genera in England,

A *Paphiopedilum* house. The adult plants are on the left hand staging, smaller ones on the right. The plant is being examined to see whether new growth has started. Note the wire netting on top of the staging to prevent a water seal forming between the base of the pot and the wood, which would prevent aeration and drainage. There are some Lily of the Amazon plants underneath the staging.

require about five years but with a little luck the first flowers will appear in four and a half; cattleyas and cymbidiums normally take five to six years; odontoglossums and miltonias about three or four years, but the plants will be small and not maximum or even optimum size before the first varieties bloom. The flowers of these precocious adults are small in size and few in number compared with those produced by a mature plant but the form and colour are identical.

There are few moments in an orchid breeder's life which match those just before the first flowers of a new cross appear. For days before, the bud has been watched in its development, precautions taken against the depredations of insects, and temperatures and humidity adjusted as never before–or rather since the last new hybrid. Slugs have an uncanny and unfortunate gift for picking out only the best buds for supper. At last the moment arrives, the flower unfolds and there is joy in the nursery or, on the other hand, weeping and wailing and gnashing of teeth, for it is a fact of orchid-breeding life that the two best parents available can be used and yet the progeny be ordinary to the point of insignificance. Since the end of the Second World War, however, the study of genetics has played an increasingly important part in orchid breeding and saved much wasted effort.

Orchid cultivation

The beginner may be confused when faced with the terms 'cool', 'intermediate', and 'hot', 'stove' or 'East India' section or house; these simply refer to the conditions required by an orchid in cultivation, particularly to the temperature and humidity. The cool house is suitable for the cymbidiums, for example, and the Mexican species found at high altitudes. The temperature in this section should not be allowed to fall below $45\,°F$ ($7\,°C$) with an average of a little above this, and there should also be a lower relative humidity, say 65 per cent. The intermediate section houses plants from the warmer climates, such as the cattleyas and their allied genera, the paphiopedilums (although some of the species can be grown in the cool house), the phalaenopses and dendrobiums and many others. It is the most crowded section. In the hot, stove, or East India section are those plants which require much more heat: Malaysian plants, such as the arandas and arachnes, some of the phalaenopses and dendrobiums, and some of the vandas. The humidity should be high—in the 80s—and the temperature also well up, with a minimum of $70\,°F$ ($21\,°C$) and an average of $80\,°F$ ($27\,°C$).

It is appropriate at this point to discuss the best way of achieving the three sections in one building. Naturally this is best done when the house is in course of construction, but any greenhouse—if it is long enough—can be adapted. In northern Europe the house should run from north to south, unless it is proposed to build a division along the whole length, in which case it should run from east to west so that there will be one side facing south, which will need to be shaded, and one side facing north which may not. The sections, if the house is not yet built, can be divided by brick walls with a door into each, but polythene sheeting will serve equally well if the greenhouse is already built. The roof should be fairly steeply pitched to ensure that drip caused by condensation runs harmlessly down and not on to the plants.

Brassavola digbyana, noted for its fimbriated labellum and for its qualities in breeding. It has been allied with *Cattleya, Sophronitis, Laelia* and most other members of the cattleya alliance.

The most important item, however, is the heating. Whether the boiler burns oil, solid fuel or gas, the piping should not be more than two inches in diameter and there should be too many pipes rather than just enough. With more, small diameter pipes the heating surface is greater in relation to the volume of water than with large diameter pipes. Although initially more expensive to install, this system is more economic to run and enables the heat to be distributed evenly throughout the house or section. Thermostats should be placed strategically—in the intermediate section and one outside the house. In addition, there could usefully be an air thermostat to work in conjunction with the intermediate section thermostat, and also a water thermostat in the boiler house. To save fuel, the outside of the house could be rendered with a waterproof compound and a damp course provided after the footings have been laid. This is because moisture conducts heat and a dry wall acts as an insulator. The inside wall, of course, must also be shielded from water, but this can be done by bringing polythene sheeting down from the plate at the top of the brickwork to the floor. Make arrangements for 'up-and-down' blinds of lath or some material such as tiffany and put the runners in place before the roof is glazed.

The best advice to a beginner consists of several points discovered during some years of experience, a period in which many mistakes were made. The first is that the benches for the plants should not be more than three feet six inches wide, for even an extra three inches will require the services of someone with the arms of an adult gorilla to lift out the plants from the back row and these, naturally, will be the ones most needed. Secondly, the rain-water tanks must be big enough and in a longish house could be placed towards each end. Water for damping down should be piped in and a stand-pipe placed in each section. Thirdly, make sure the ventilators are large enough and that the side vents are completely airtight when closed.

All these things cost money, but they make for economy in the long run and a quieter and more contented orchid-growing life.

The genera most popular for glasshouse cultivation because of their adaptability to artificial climatic conditions are *Cattleya* and allied genera, *Cymbidium, Odontoglossum, Miltonia* and *Paphiopedilum.*

The cultivation of *Cattleya* and its allied genera has been carried on very successfully in England for nearly 150 years, and these genera are now worldwide in popularity. The species from which the hybrids are descended are distributed over Central and South America—Brazil and Colombia are particularly rich fields for laelias and cattleyas—and the little scarlet *Sophronitis grandiflora,* which gave the suffusion of colour to its larger cousins, also comes from Brazil. The first hybrid cattleya to flower, *C. hybrida,* was lost but *C. brabantiae* flowered soon after in 1863, and was the first hybrid orchid to gain an award from the R.H.S., a Silver Banksian Medal.

In addition to the laelias, the next most important allied genus so far used in hybridization is *Brassavola* although, like *Sophronitis,* it was generally used many generations of hybrids ago. It is similar, too, in that one species in particular was selected by the pioneers in hybridization for interbreeding, and this was *Brassavola digbyana,* discovered in Mexico, British

Braziliana: orchids, bromeliads, ferns, waterplants all grow in profusion. Many of the orchid species grown in cultivation have their natural habitat in this type of steamy Amazonian jungle.

Cattleya guatemalensis. This fragrant, pale
rose orchid is interesting because it is a
natural hybrid between *C. skinneri* and
aurantiaca (which was formerly classified as
an *Epidendrum*).

Honduras and Guatemala. It is noted for its magnificent fringed
lip, the rest of the flower, pale green in colour, not being
particularly striking. The influence of *B. digbyana* is seen to this
day in the delicate fimbriations of the labellum of the brassolaelio-
cattleyas and the potinaras.

Cattleyas are orchids for the intermediate house, with the
exception of those *Cattleya* and *Laelia* species originating from
the hills of Mexico or Colombia which need cooler temperatures.
Briefly, the *Cattleya* alliance requires warmth, light and humidity
in rather different proportions from what are needed by other
commercial orchids, and although many amateur growers have
been very successful in housing the different genera in one house,
it is better and easier to divide the house, if large enough – and
quite small houses are adaptable – into separate sections for intermediate and cool-house orchids. This may easily be done by
using a plastic such as polythene tacked on to a lath framework.

In nature the species grow in conditions where it is wet for
periods of months at a time followed by periods of drought, so
the watering of cattleyas is therefore of great importance to the
health of the plant, as the early orchid growers learnt by bitter
experience. Too much watering can cause poor growth and
eventually death, usually because the roots rot away. During the
period of growth, which starts in the early spring when the first
new roots push their way out from the base of the front of the
plant and the new growth shows its green tip, water may be given
according to the state of the compost. When this is dry the plant
is ready to be watered. It cannot be stressed too often that the
worst thing to do, in a mistaken belief that the plant appreciates
it, is to dribble a little water daily into the pot; when the time
comes saturate the compost, if necessary by plunging the pot into
a bucket of water.

It must always be kept in mind that cattleyas are epiphytic and
in consequence their leaves play a major part in absorbing
nourishment, and that their ancestral home is in the dense forests
of the Amazon basin, the jungles of Central and South America
and the wooded foothills of Costa Rica and other tropical
American countries. Although the jungles at ground level are
very humid, there is progressively less moisture in the air at
higher levels, and this is where the cattleyas flourish. Owing to
the heat the humidity of the lower strata rises and passes out of
the area of trees to dissipate itself in the air above; the cattleyas,
therefore, are always in moving air containing moisture. These
conditions are easily copied in a greenhouse by means of 'damping down', which simply means spraying water over the paths,
walls and benches, in fact on everything except the plants. At the
same time, the provision of fans to keep the air moving is another
step towards natural growing. Also, there should always be
plenty of space between the pots on the staging to allow light and
air to reach as much of the plant as possible.

In temperate climates the factor which is most difficult to
provide adequately in growing all tropical orchids is that of light,
and here northern European growers are greatly handicapped.
To provide a high enough intensity of light during the winter,
when it is dark at three o'clock in the afternoon and never really
light at any time, would tax the financial resources of a Croesus,
and consequently most commercial orchids are grown for only

A fine example of a variety of *Cymbidium* Balkis. This hybrid has now superceded Alexanderi, Westonbirt variety, F.C.C., R.H.S., for breeding purposes.

half the year. The ideal temperatures for cattleyas in such climates during the winter are 60°F (16°C) by day and 55°F (13°C) by night and they require summer temperatures of 70–75°F (21–24°C) during the day and 65°F (18°C) at night. As a consequence of the decrease in daylight the amount of humidity needed is less, and watering is much less necessary because there is less evaporation from the surface of the compost.

Hard scale is the most important of the pests and diseases to which cattleyas are vulnerable. It is brought in from nearby trees through ventilators open in the late summer, and thrives – as do most orchid pests – in hot dry conditions, which is a very good reason for keeping the humidity up. Aphids also thrive in hot dry conditions and occasionally attack individual plants. Thrips used to be a scourge, but can now be controlled by various insecticides. A routine treatment with a good systemic insecticide will effectively control scale and most other pests. There should be two treatments at intervals of ten days or so, and then another two in three or four months.

Although most cattleya hybrids are tidy growers there are exceptions. All plants must be properly staked at the right time to give them a neat appearance and to encourage them to grow to the best advantage. They are easier to manage if they are tidy: they can be watered more easily and efficiently and the circulation of air has greater effect.

The Mexican species are treated differently as, because of their origin in the higher terrain of Mexico and Colombia, they require less moisture and even more light than the hybrids. Probably the best way of growing them is to hang them in baskets or established on slabs of bark or pieces of fibre near the glass roof. This has two effects, firstly they derive more light and secondly they are not likely to suffer from overwatering as it is such a bother to get them down for dunking in a bucket of water.

To sum up, cattleyas require as much light as possible at all times of the year but in summer the leaves must not be allowed to become warm to the touch; they require as much water as they will take to saturate the compost and must then be left severely alone; and the heating must be genial and not fierce. It is better to have a temperature lower by five degrees than to have the theoretically correct one with an unpleasant dry feeling in the atmosphere.

The *Cymbidium* genus is treated in a similar manner to *Cattleya,* but with one or two important differences.

Cymbidiums are widely distributed throughout the Far East and grow at an average height of 5,000 feet. *Cymbidium giganteum* is one of the most widely dispersed of the genus and grows at altitudes from 1,000 feet in Sikkim up to 5,500 feet. At Kollong, one of the places where it is found, the rainfall from April to November is about ninety inches and the daily temperature is 65–70°F (18–21°C), rarely rising to 80°F (27°C); from November to April the season is almost rainless and the temperature in January and February falls to below 32°F (0°C) nearly every night. At Sikkim, the rainfall during the same period reaches almost one hundred and fifty inches and in the summer months the temperature often rises to 90°F (32°C), while the winter months are not quite rainless and the temperature never falls to freezing point. These figures give a good idea of the sort of country in which cymbidiums flourish, and in particular it emphasizes the fact that at the average height of 5,000 feet the plants are always enveloped in low cloud and mist during the wet season.

Sir Joseph Hooker who, in collaboration with Dr Thompson, collected the delightful miniature *C. devonianum,* described the natural habitat of cymbidiums in his *Himalayan Journals,* 1849–51, 'though freely exposed to the sun and the winds, dews and frost, rain and droughts, they were all fresh, bright green and strong under very different treatment from that to which they are exposed in the damp, unhealthy, steamy orchid houses of our English gardens'.

Although the first *Cymbidium* species to be imported into England was *C. pendulum,* with its pendulous inflorescence of pale yellow, purple-striped flowers, it was not at all typical of the generality of the other species, and, in common with

C. aloifolium (Burma), *C. canaliculatum* (northern and eastern Australia to New South Wales), *C. finlaysonianum* (Malaysia) of the leathery leaves, the early-flowering *C. lancifolium* (India, Malaysia and Japan), which has pale green, scented flowers, and several others, it requires warmer conditions than the vast majority of the genus which, owing to the cool and moist surroundings of their natural habitat, appreciate a cool, moist atmosphere.

In 1899 the first hybrid was raised by Veitch between *C. eburneum* and *C. lowianum* and named *C. eburneolowianum*. The modern hybrids are descended from *Cymbidium* species such as the very fragrant *C. eburneum* with waxy, ivory-white flowers, *C. parishii-sanderae*, which has large white scented flowers and is now very rare, *C. insigne* with large white flowers suffused with rose-lilac, perhaps the most important ancestor of modern hybrid cymbidiums, and *C. lowianum* with arching spikes three feet long, sometimes bearing as many as three dozen large green flowers. These orchids come mostly from the Himalayas and the Khasia Hills. The most distinguished *Cymbidium* hybrid ever raised – distinguished because it was such an advance on its predecessors – was *C.* Alexanderi, Westonbirt variety, which received a First Class Certificate from the Royal Horticultural Society over fifty years ago. The *Orchid Review* described it at the time as, 'the largest and finest variety so far raised. The robust plant bore a couple of spikes with an aggregate of twelve ivory-white flowers, the lip mottled with mauve . . .' Not only is it an outstanding form, even today, but it has proved to be a wonderful parent, which is not always the case with outstanding forms of cymbidiums or, for that matter, of any other genera. It is in the pedigree of hundreds of the best hybrids of today.

It has been discovered in recent years that the temperatures in which cymbidiums thrive in glasshouses are perhaps a little warmer than is generally recommended, though harm is usually done by too high a temperature in the daytime in summer. A winter night temperature of 50–55°F (10–13°C) is better than the minimum of 45°F (7°C), and a day temperature of 60–63°F (16–17°C) is better than 55°F (13°C). Summer temperatures of 60°F (16°C) at night and 65–70°F (18–21°C) during the day are the optimum, but sometimes it is impossible to restrain the day temperature when the outside one is soaring into the high eighties. When this occurs, a quick spraying of the foliage with a coarse spoon rose or some other appliance is necessary. There ought always to be a difference of 10–15°F (5–8°C) between the day and night temperatures.

Like the cattleyas, cymbidiums require rather special watering, but the drying-out need not be so thorough. They also love as much light as is possible without causing the leaves to be warm to the touch, and plenty of air round the plant. The pots must be spaced well away from each other, even though precious bench-space is needed for other plants. Give as much air as possible during the growing season and if ventilators wide open are not sufficient, fans should be installed. These, together with copious damping down during all but the coolest days, will give the plants the conditions to which their ancestors were used.

If the humidity is kept high at all times, pests and diseases will not be the menace they are when too much heat and not enough moisture occur. Red spider mite is the worst enemy, and a routine treatment with any one of the several excellent systemic insecticides available will control it. These pests, like most of the scourges of orchids, love arid conditions and come into the house airborne from neighbouring trees.

When the happiest time of the *Cymbidium* year approaches and flower buds show themselves at the base of the pseudobulbs, a stake should be put into each pot as soon as the bud is discovered. A forest of stakes is not only a good guide to where the flowering plants are but is a splendid sight for the grower, being the shape of things to come.

The *Odontoglossum* genus has always been a favourite with English growers and hybridizers from the very earliest days of the importation and then the hybridization of orchids. Although there are hundreds of species and subspecies, very few were originally used in hybridization, and of these few, *Odontoglossum crispum* is by far the most popular, both in its own right and also as a breeding plant. There are over sixty varieties of this most beautiful white orchid listed in *Sander's Orchid Guide, 1927*. The variations are usually of the different spotting and blotching. *O. pescatorei*, *O. harryanum*, *O. triumphans* and *O. luteo-purpureum* are also in the pedigree of many of the finest hybrids of today. *O. harryanum*, which was named in honour of Sir Harry Veitch, is dark chestnut-brown streaked with yellow. Since so few species were used as parents the fine forms of the present-day odontoglossum are the result of very selective breeding, only the best from each generation being used as parents.

Although several attempts were made to send live odontoglossums back to England, none was successful until Ure-Skinner collected *O. bictoniense* in Guatemala in 1835, and the first hybrid of this genus was not raised and flowered until the turn of the century. This flower was first discovered in the

A pre-war *Cymbidium* house. Note the large 'open' flowers and the curved edge of the panes of glass indicating the antiquity of the house. Over 100 years old, it is one of the orchid houses originally built for the firm of Veitch and Sons. The curved edge allows rain on the outside and condensation on the inside to run down the centre of the panes thus avoiding rot in the wooden frames.

Odontoglossum grande from Mexico and Guatemala is the largest-flowered of the *Odontoglossum* species, the blooms being more than six inches across. It was first discovered by Ure-Skinner in 1839.

collection of Sir Trevor Lawrence at Burford Lodge, Dorking; Reichenbach suggested that it might possibly be a natural hybrid between the white *O. pescatorei* and *O. triumphans,* golden-yellow barred with chestnut-brown, and when Seden of Veitch's made the cross between these two species the progeny proved the professor to have been right. The most popular *Odontoglossum* species cultivated at the present time are, among others, *crispum* (Colombia), *citrosmum* (Mexico), *cervantesii* (Mexico) a small-growing, rose-coloured species with concentric dark red circles, *rossii* (Mexico), *pescatorei* (Colombia), *hallii* (Ecuador and Peru), and *grande* (Guatemala), the largest species of all, having huge yellow flowers patterned with red. Their flowering periods are spread throughout the year, and hybrids can also be found in flower in most months except July and August.

The cultivation of odontoglossums involves a high humidity, a moist compost at all times, a buoyant atmosphere, no feeling of fire heat from the pipes, and extra shading during the summer. The optimum summer temperatures are 65°F (18°C) during the day and 60°F (16°C) at night, and during the winter 60°F (16°C) by day and 50°F (10°C) at night.

Like the cattleyas, odontoglossums intercross readily with several other genera—with *Miltonia* to make a bigeneric hybrid named *Odontonia* and with *Cochlioda* to form *Odontioda. Cochlioda* is a small genus of about half a dozen brilliantly coloured species distributed over Peru, Colombia and Ecuador. The brilliant orange-scarlet *C. noezliana* is the species most generally used for breeding. A trigeneric hybrid between *Odontoglossum, Miltonia* and *Cochlioda* is called *Vuylstekeara,* and a quadrigeneric hybrid between these three genera plus *Oncidium* is called *Wilsonara.* Fine hybrids have also been made with *Odontoglossum* and *Oncidium* alone to produce *Odontocidium.*

Many orchid lovers are attracted to paphiopedilums by the curious shape and often striking markings of their flowers. They belong to a genus distributed throughout most of Asia at altitudes ranging from 6,000 feet almost to sea level but always in areas of high humidity and warmth at all times.

There are two main divisions of this genus: from the grower's viewpoint they can be simply stated as those with plain green foliage and those with tessellated or mottled leaves. The latter species usually need more warmth than the plain-leaved in greenhouse cultivation, and are placed at the 'boiler-end' of the house. If some of the mottled-leaved species are listed here with their place of origin the reason for their need for warmth is immediately apparent: *Paphiopedilum argus* (Philippines), *P. barbatum* (Malacca), *P. bellatulum* (Thailand and Burma), a very wonderful species with a large, almost completely circular flower but hardly any stem, *P. callosum* (Thailand), *P. ciliolare* (Malaysia), *P. concolor* (Burma), *P. godefroyae* (Java), *P. niveum* (Langkawi Islands and Borneo) and *P. lawrenceanum* (Borneo). The plain-leaved *Paphiopedilum* species are found in similar geographical locations, but their habitat is much higher and therefore cooler.

The first species to be brought to England was *P. venustum.* This is white suffused with green and striped with purple, and was discovered by Dr Wallich at Sylhet in north-eastern India in 1819. It was used as a parent when the art of hybridization

One of the early shows held by the British Orchid Growers' Association in the Old Hall of the Royal Horticultural Society. These shows have been held each March since 1950.

Odontoglossum crispum, the most prolific parent in the *Odontoglossum* alliance. Even as long ago as 1946 it had been crossed with nearly 300 odontoglossums and species from other genera.

Below: A group of cattleyas and allied genera displaying the great diversity of colour and form shown by this alliance

Cymbidium Leslie Greenwood, a modern hybrid showing a desirable green shade. From Flowers of the World by Frances Perry which is illustrated by the artist for whom this orchid is named.

A Vanda coerulea hybrid. V. coerulea, the Blue Orchid beloved of the Victorians, has been used frequently by hybridists in the Far East and Hawaii.

became generally practised, and the first hybrid paphiopedilum to flower was shown by Veitch at Chelsea in 1869; it was a cross between *villosum* and *barbatum* and was named *Harrisianum* in honour of Mr Harris, John Dominy's mentor. *P. villosum,* glossy dark brownish-red tinged in places with pale green and purple, was very often used as a parent during the early years of hybridization, together with the yellowish-green *P. insigne* – the most popular of all, because of its many fine varieties – *P. spicerianum* and *P. boxallii;* others used less frequently were species such as *bellatulum, druryi, curtisii* and *fairieanum.*

Although paphiopedilums are often regarded as cool-house orchids – and, of course, some of the species are – it has been discovered by specialists in their culture that they do better in the intermediate house. Optimum temperatures during the summer are 70–75°F (21–24°C) in the daytime and 60–65°F (16–18°C) at night, and during the winter a daytime temperature of 60–65°F (16–18°C) and 55–60°F (13–16°C) at night. Owing to their ancestral habitats in the monsoon belt, they need warmth with a high humidity day and night, and must be given far less light than the other genera. Quite heavy shading in summer is essential, the glass being cleaned in the late autumn. Because of their modest light needs, the paphiopedilums – compared with cymbidiums and cattleyas, for instance – are perhaps less at a disadvantage vis-a-vis those grown commercially in more favoured climates.

The potting compost at present consists of a mixture of sphagnum moss peat, live sphagnum moss, and an 'opening' ingredient such as expanded polystyrene or charcoal. Fir bark has also been used in England with marked success. Re-potting of hybrids is done during the early spring to give the plants a long growing season. During re-potting, the plants may easily be divided.

After the plants have been re-potted in moist compost they must never be allowed to dry out completely, as is necessary for the cattleya alliance and, to a lesser degree, the cymbidiums. The watering is more trouble than with these two genera and the plants should be 'looked at' every day; those which show the slightest sign of drying-out must be given a little water and the others left severely alone. The live sphagnum moss in the compost will start to grow if conditions are correct and this moss is a very good watering indicator in that it turns pale in colour when becoming dry, and white when completely dry.

Unlike cattleyas and cymbidiums, the paphiopedilums are gregarious, and like to be close to each other. This is a reminder they they are terrestrial plants. Ventilation is necessary only on the hottest days. Although the optimum temperature in the summer is between 70°F and 75°F (21°C and 24°C) no harm will ensue if it goes up to 90°F (32°C), the old trick of feeling the leaves for warmth coming into play once more.

If the plants are staked as soon as the bud appears it will enable the flower to grow correctly; these blooms are so heavy that unless the flower stem is commensurately thick – as it is in many species – it will not grow erect.

There are few diseases or pests which attack paphiopedilums under glass and they are relatively innocuous. The high humidity and the moist surface of the compost seem to deter those pests

Phalaenopsis schilleriana, a delicate rose-purple suffused with white, was named after Consul Schiller of Hamburg who sent it home from Manila in 1858. It has been used successfully in hybridization in recent years.

Odontoglossum Edalvo, a delicately coloured *Odontoglossum* hybrid flowered several years ago, is typical of this genus.

Paphiopedilum concolor is very difficult to grow successfully in England. Its natural habitat is rocky hollows filled with decaying vegetable matter, and also limestone cliffs facing the sea in the Birds' Nests' Islands in South-east Asia.

Paphiopedilum venustum is one of the easiest of all orchids to cultivate and thrives well in living room conditions.

Odontoglossum triumphans grows at heights of 5,000–10,000 feet. It is a useful species in north temperate greenhouses because it flowers from March to May when not many other orchids are in flower.

which thrive in hot, dry conditions, and the moss fly and occasionally the springtail are easily controlled by any of the insecticides containing BHC.

In addition to the genera already described there are others—such as *Phalaenopsis, Vanda* and *Dendrobium*—which can be grown successfully under glass, although, because of the expense involved in providing sufficient heat, they are probably most popular among orchidologists who are lucky enough to live in climates where they can be cultivated in the open.

Many of the most attractive species of *Phalaenopsis,* for example, are found in habitats with high temperatures and high humidity. *P. boxalli,* yellow with red-brown bars and blotches, *P. schilleriana,* rose-purple with the sepals dotted with a darker purple, and *P. luedemanniana*, a very bright species with sepals and petals having alternate bars of pale yellow, chestnut-brown and amethyst-purple, all come from the Philippines; the deciduous *P. lowii*, rose-coloured with a reddish midrib, comes from Burma; while the pale yellow-green *P. cornu-cervi*, a species used in hybridizing to obtain varieties of a different colour, comes from Malaysia and Burma.

As may be expected, phalaenopses in cultivation require warmth and humidity. In summer the day temperature should be 75–80°F (24–27°C) and 70°F (21°C) at night; winter temperatures may be a little less, 65–70°F (18–21°C) during the day, and 60–65°F (16–18°C) at night. Because they need a humidity near saturation point, there will not be such a high rate of evaporation and as a consequence watering should be infrequent; it is important that the surface of the compost only should be watered, not the foliage. As drainage is critical, the plants do best in open baskets or on rafts of fibre or bark. They do not like *full* sunlight and will therefore be happy in a warm part of the paphiopedilum house.

The species which make up the genus *Vanda* are found in widely varying natural habitats. For example, *V. amesiana,* white flushed with rose-purple, grows at an altitude of about 4,000 feet with the temperature varying from about 36–65°F (2–18°C) during the flowering period; in contrast *V. bensonii,* yellowish-green veined with chestnut, was discovered by Colonel Benson on deciduous trees quite unprotected from the sun during the dry season, a time when the temperature rises to 112°F (45°C) in the shade. *V. tricolor,* a Javanese species introduced by Thomas Lobb in 1846, has yellowish-white flowers spotted with red-brown and is found growing on large trees at 1,500–2,500 feet. *V. tricolor* var. *suavis* is a beautiful form with sepals and petals of white, spotted and barred with red-purple. *V. teres,* a species with cylindrical stem and leaves, is rosy-purple suffused with white and is found in hot plains and valleys exposed to full sun in India, Assam and Burma.

Because the species are found in nature in such divergent conditions—from cool to very hot—their treatment in greenhouses must also vary, but there are one or two cultural common denominators. The plants must have all the light possible without scorching the leaves, the compost must be extremely open to allow of first class drainage and aeration, and water must not be allowed to lodge in the axils of the leaves. In other words, the cultivation is similar to that employed in the growing of

Phalaenopsis Jane Alnquist, a recent *Phalaenopsis* hybrid of good modern form; that is, the flowers are rounder and fatter in shape than in early hybrids. It is part of a group, which includes among other genera many cymbidiums, displayed at one of the British Orchid Growers' Association shows.

phalaenopses. *V. coerulea* can be grown in much cooler temperatures, especially winter night temperatures, while *V. teres* must have warmth at all times and be grown near the glass with a night temperature about ten degrees below that of the daytime. All the species of this genus must be kept moist at all times, but less so during the resting period.

Many of the 1,500 or so species of *Dendrobium* are of botanical or scientific interest only, but there are many attractive species in a wide range of colours which can be cultivated. *D. atro-violaceum* is cream with purple blotches and a violet lip; *D. brymerianum*, golden-yellow, was introduced by Low and Co. in 1874, while the magenta-purple *D. bigibbum* from Australia—the lip is darker—was flowered at Kew as early as 1824. *D. chryso-toxum*, rich golden-yellow with an orange lip, is distributed over the plains and mountains of Lower Burma, being found at altitudes of 3,000 feet at its highest. The deep orange *D. fimbriatum* was discovered by Wallich in Nepal; its variety *occulatum*, sent to Chatsworth by Gibson in 1837, is very generally cultivated. The flowers are smaller than the type and there is a large maroon-red blotch on the lip. The Australian species *D. kingianum* is violet-purple shaded with white and *D. nobile*, perhaps the most popular of the dendrobes, is whiteish at the base of the segments, which are tipped with amethyst-purple, and has a rich maroon-purple disc on the lip. It comes from southern China, the north and north-east of India and Formosa.

The cultivation of this genus depends on the type of habitat and climate in which a particular species is found. The rule common to most is that during the growing season they should be given plenty of moisture; those plants growing on rafts or in baskets should be dipped in tepid water two or three times a week and those in pots watered well once a week. All should be lightly syringed twice a day, morning and evening. When the growths are 'made up'—or fully matured—the plants should then be given cooler, dryer treatment in order to harden the growths and as much light as possible within reason. They should be watered very sparingly. *D. atro-violaceum, D. bigibbum* and *D. kingianum* should be given a little more water than the Indian and Burmese species during this resting, or rather maturing, period. The night temperatures should be 55–60°F (13–16°C) for most of the Indian and Burmese species and those growing at high altitudes, and 60–65°F (16–18°C) during the day. At all times there must be a genial, buoyant atmosphere, that is, with no hint of fire heat. In northern Europe shading during the bright sunny days of July and August should be applied from two hours after sunrise to two hours before sunset. The compost should always be open and well-drained.

There remains one aspect of cultivation which might one day be the commonplace method of growing certain genera commercially. This is bed-culture and would apply particularly to the cut-flower trade. Cymbidiums have for many years been grown successfully in beds; this method has many advantages and few disadvantages, the most important of which is the fear that if disease attacks one or two plants it will run through the whole bed. This danger could easily be prevented by partitioning the bed, so that one section only would be lost. There is no reason

Dendrobium nobile, with a distribution from northern India to southern China, is probably the most popular dendrobium in cultivation and has given its name to a group of *Dendrobium* hybrids. It is recorded that Mr Rucker of Wandsworth possessed a variety which bore over 1,000 blooms at the same time.

Vanda Miss Joachim *(V. hookeriana x V. teres,* 1893) is the oldest and one of the most successful of *Vanda* hybrids. It is very popular in the cut flower industry in Hawaii.

why other terrestrial orchids such as paphiopedilums should not be grown in a similar manner since the ground is, after all, their natural element. In northern Italy the growers of *P. insigne* for the Christmas cut-flower market have been doing this successfully for years, so why is it not attempted with hybrids? Just as present methods are very different from those of the past, it is probable that the future will see even greater changes.

Since the end of the Second World War, the character of orchid growing has changed dramatically. Although growers no longer send travellers to the tropical jungles of the world for the purpose of collecting orchid species, these species have been exported by the producing countries to other countries all over the world. For instance, orchid species are collected, packed and despatched by specialists in Colombia, Peru, Guatemala, Mexico, India, Malaysia, Thailand, Japan and Formosa. The main markets for these exports are northern Europe, including Great Britain, and the U.S.A. Although the torrent of species of the last century has ceased, there are still orchid collectors and firms who confine their purchases to species rather than hybrids, and often to species of one genus. These are sometimes re-exported after having been established and grown for a year.

The export of orchid plants from English growers has been the main part of the total sales of many commercial growers ever since the early 1920s, when the chief markets for English hybrids were the U.S.A. firstly, then Australia, and South Africa, Ceylon, Singapore, and Malaysia. All these countries had—and continue to have—orchid societies or clubs, most with first-class periodicals dealing solely with orchid matters. So important to English growers was their world export trade that anything affecting it adversely, such as regulations imposed by an importing country restricting the inward flow of orchid plants, was critical to their survival, and in February 1948, the British Orchid Growers' Association was formed. The Association consisted of commercial growers only and for the first few years of its life was very busy dealing with matters affecting the export of orchids. For example, it dealt directly with the Ministry of Agriculture, the Board of Trade and the Export Council in England and their counterparts in the U.S.A. and Australia, as a result of which the export of orchids was carried on smoothly. The air freight rates to Australia were the heaviest, naturally, and combined shipments were regularly arranged by which low commodity rates were achieved with a consequent saving to the exporters.

In addition to their export business, British growers were very concerned to see the home market rise once more to significant proportions. With the imposition of wartime restrictions and the shortages after the war only the very largest amateur collections managed to survive; publicity was directed at making orchids known to a new generation by means of talks, exhibits at great international shows in the U.S.A., Australia, Singapore and the European Floralies Ghentoises, and the organization of annual B.O.G.A. Shows, culminating in the Third World Orchid Conference. Their success is apparent in the number of orchid societies now in existence throughout the country.

The U.S.A. now leads the world in many aspects of orchidology, a position built up gradually since the end of the Second World War. With the unequalled advantages of the great range

Cymbidiums growing under a lath canopy in Madeira. This is similar to the way in which they are grown in southern California and New South Wales.

of climate, from the high temperatures and high humidity of Florida to the temperate climate of North Carolina and the more extreme climates of New England and the Pacific north-west, it would have been indeed remarkable if the U.S.A. had not become pre-eminent in output—and in range and variety—of orchids.

The Mediterranean-type climate of southern California is equable enough to be ideal for the growing of, say, cymbidiums without artificial heat, while orchid growers in other states must use glasshouses provided with heat to a greater or lesser degree. The most favourable district is that almost mid-way between San Francisco and Los Angeles, where acres of cymbidium plants are cultivated under lath-roofed constructions, open at the sides most of the time. Other genera such as cattleyas or paphiopedilums need to be grown in glasshouses with a little heat at some periods of the year. In Florida, round Miami, and at the other side, round St Petersburg, cattleyas can be grown outside, although many growers do have a greenhouse. If, however, a plant does not flourish in the greenhouse, the cure is to fix it to the top of a convenient palm tree—and there is always a convenient palm tree—after which treatment the cattleya recovers and eventually thrives.

There are huge establishments all over the U.S.A., from Connecticut and New York to the southernmost states, which have a tremendous trade in cut flowers, particularly cymbidiums and cattleyas; there is now a growing taste for the long-neglected paphiopedilum, neglected perhaps because there is only a single flower on a plant compared with the twenty produced by a cymbidium. These cut-flower specialists send their blooms to markets all over the country by air freight, which is much less expensive than in European countries. The queen of all the areas for production of orchid plants as well as cut flowers must be Hawaii, for if the mainland U.S.A. has a great range of climate spread over thousands of miles, Hawaii has an equal range in a much more concentrated area.

Along with an energetic industry the U.S.A. also has a seemingly inexhaustible domestic market, and the number of enthusiastic amateurs all over the country, banded together in clubs and societies and headed by the American Orchid Society, must be staggering to a European. The universities, with their laboratory expertise, are often brought into the picture for technical advice and for co-operation in experiments, sometimes to do with plant physiology and sometimes to do with the control of pests and disease. The one disadvantage about having a wonderful growing climate for plants is that it is frequently equally advantageous for insects, microbes and fungi, but even this provides an incentive to find the control, research which would otherwise be less urgent.

Australia has a range of climate almost equal to that of the U.S.A. and also a great number of native orchids of great scientific interest, and many of horticultural worth. The classic work describing these is *Orchids of Australia* by W. H. Nicholls, 1969, which is overwhelming in its detail and contains nearly 500 colour plates reproduced from paintings by the author. The paintings are exquisite and the text highly scientific; this book is probably the finest produced since the war, if not since the

A fine display of cymbidiums growing in the open. This is only possible in those parts of the world favoured with a warm climate.

beginning of the century, on regional orchids.

New South Wales, with a Mediterranean type of climate, is probably the most favoured growing area; the ubiquitous cymbidium is cultivated there with the facility of those grown in southern California, and the cut-flower industry is flourishing, blooms being exported to many parts of the world, including Britain (which does not impose import restrictions). They arrive in England during the period when English cymbidiums are not in flower, from September up to about November, and are handled by Covent Garden market. The adjacent state of Victoria, with its cooler climate necessitating the employment of glasshouses and some heating, is ideal for the cultivation of those genera grown under glass in northern Europe, such as cymbidiums, paphiopedilums, odontoglossums and the cattleya alliance. Queensland, an elongated state from south to north and the home of the Cooktown Orchid (*Dendrobium bigibbum*)–the floral emblem of Queensland–has a greater range of temperatures than the other states, and the northern part, where the Cooktown Orchid is found, is suitable for the cultivation of the warmer-growing genera. In the south, there is a vigorous community of amateur orchid growers, and genera such as *Cattleya, Dendrobium* and *Phalaenopsis* are popular.

It is natural that in such good orchid-growing conditions there should be vigorous orchid societies and, headed by the national organization, the Australian Orchid Council, there are clubs and societies in New South Wales, Queensland, Victoria, South Australia, Western Australia and Tasmania.

Malaysia is probably the foremost exporting country in the Far East, with thousands of cut flowers being sent to European markets every year. These orchids come from genera which because of their heating and lighting requirements can only be grown in northern Europe at great cost, an uneconomic venture, wonderful though their blooms are. But in addition to growing orchids for export, there are enthusiastic amateur growers in all countries where these beautiful orchids are indigenous and much new hybridization is at present being carried out.

Orchids in the living room

In temperate climates the greenhouse has long been the natural home for orchids cultivated in artificial conditions, but for nearly as many years they have been grown with varying degrees of success in living rooms and conservatories heated by the same system as that of the dwelling house, often open fires burning coal or wood. Since the arrival of central heating, the provision of heat—one of the most important factors in the cultivation of orchids—is no longer the problem it once was when open or gas fires were the most usual means of warming a small- to medium-sized dwelling house.

It was much more difficult in the old days, but even so there were many people who made a triumph of this method of orchid-growing. The dust, inseparable from the burning of wood or coal, was carefully sponged from the foliage of the plants at regular weekly intervals; this had the dual effect of improving both the appearance of the plants and their growing efficiency by keeping the stomata from becoming clogged, and the small amount of moisture was also beneficial to the orchids. The conditions, although not ideal, could have been worse, and one benefit of solid fuel heating was that the fires were allowed to die down or to go out at night and were relit each morning. There was thus an automatic lowering of the night temperature.

In a modern house having either gas or oil-fired boilers, or one of the several methods of electric central heating, thermo-static control is normal; the temperature of individual rooms is often regulated by means of motorized valves and, in any case, many householders programme their heating to be lower at night. Such houses are eminently suitable for an attempt at the cultivation of orchids.

Apart from heating, there are two other main factors to be considered: light and humidity. In their natural habitat orchids have at least twelve hours light every day, sometimes light of great intensity and sometimes a more subdued light. The difference depends on the kind of orchid and whether it grows at the top of a tree or whether it lives in shady conditions on the

Miltonia Red Knight var. Grail, A.M., R.H.S., the finest miltonia so far shown for form, colour and size

Miniature cymbidiums are ideal for the gardener with limited space in his greenhouse or for the living-room grower.

ground. Some Brazilian species such as *Cattleya bicolor* belong to the first group and *Paphiopedilum lawrenceanum,* for example, is one of the shade-lovers.

While it is relatively easy to provide adequate heat and light, humidity is more difficult. The humidity of the jungle is high at all times, and even the Mexican species, which are undemanding as regards watering–at least during certain periods of their growth cycle–do grow in conditions of high humidity. It would be impractical to provide this kind of atmosphere in an entire living room, the plants would love it but the curtains, carpets and other furnishings would rapidly begin to rot. There are several ways of introducing humidity to plants at no detriment to the furnishing fabrics of the room which are described later.

Although heat and light are essential, too much of either can be inhibiting to the health and well-being of the plants. A site near a window is best, but even in northern Europe a south window is possible only in winter because such a situation would grow too hot in summer. In more favoured climates, such as California, Natal or New South Wales, a window facing east is probably the best site, so that the orchids can benefit from the early morning warmth and light without being scorched by the mid-day heat. A constant circulation of air is also very necessary as most orchids enjoy light airy conditions.

From the foregoing it is obvious that a constant removal of the plants from one site to another, depending on the time of year or day, is one way of ensuring the maximum opportunity for the plants to thrive. However, by the use of ingenuity and a little finance most rooms are capable of containing a nook devoted more or less permanently to orchids. Hundreds of contented growers in every part of the U.S.A. have met the challenge and, often after a long struggle, have succeeded in finding out the right way of handling orchid plants in their own living rooms. In Canada, too, there are many enthusiastic orchid growers living in apartments whose hobby has been 'learnt the hard way'.

In order to provide orchids with conditions as close to their needs as possible, extra light in the form of fluorescent tubes suspended a foot or eighteen inches above the plants can be used to extend the hours of daylight to the optimum, and in winter they can be left on during the day to give added light to the weak, wintry daylight. Orchid plants require at least ten hours of darkness in order that the process of growing may be properly balanced. Plants take in carbon dioxide during the daylight hours and use this during the hours of darkness to increase the multiplication of cells. In nature the tropical day is divided into twelve hours of light and twelve hours of darkness. This balance varies slightly as the sun moves from the Equator to the tropic of Cancer in the north or of Capricorn in the south, but there are always at least ten hours of dark. Temperate regions are usually either at great altitudes when situated between the tropics or completely outside the tropic and subtropic zones. Orchid growing indoors is most general in the temperate parts of the world–in the tropics and subtropics outside cultivation is possible. It is possible, indeed desirable, to combine the two, literally to have the best of both worlds by wintering the plants in the living room and putting them outside during the late spring, summer and early autumn to reap the benefits of sun-

Laelia gouldiana, a natural hybrid between *autumnalis* and *anceps*, is one of the easiest and most attractive of all orchids and suitable either for the living-room or for the cool house.

light unfiltered by glass and, if in a suitable area, of clean rain and pure air. The most successful growers follow this routine. Often a cellar or basement is used for growing the plants, and the orchids never see the light of day until they are given their yearly holiday-in-the-sun.

Most centrally-heated rooms have the radiators situated under a window and, depending on which way the window faces, this is the best position to site the 'orchid house'. If the window is in an alcove or is a bay window, so much the better. First a flat surface such as a metal (preferably zinc) tray should be fixed over the radiator to hold a moisture-retaining material – gravel, broken brick or crocks, for example – and the orchid plants placed on top of inverted flower pots on this tray. The wet gravel, acting as a buffer between the radiator and plants, receives and vaporizes the heat from the radiator and this vapour rising past the plants gives them the humidity they need. The whole bay window or alcove can be glassed in with sliding glass or plastic doors to give easy access to the plants for watering and general handling, but some provision should be made for ventilation at the top and bottom either by means of louvres or perforations in the glass or plastic; if these are not sufficient to allow a controlled flow of air a small fan could be

Left: Lycaste cruenta, a beautiful species from Guatemala with larger but fewer flowers than *L. aromatica*

Dendrobium aggregatum growing in a freely movable stand, an example of a well-grown, living-room orchid

Bottom: Lycaste Auburn, a hybrid with a strange form in which the sepals are much larger than the petals.

employed. The outside window should be double-glazed and there should be some means of manipulating the blinds at night or during the day when the sun is too strong.

There is an enthusiastic orchid society in Helsinki, Finland, where indoor orchid-growing has been practised for thirty to forty years, although the society has not been formed for quite so long. Many years ago, before central heating was generally introduced, orchids such as *Coelogyne cristata, Paphiopedilum insigne* and *Odontoglossum grande* were the most popular because they bloomed freely in the conditions prevailing at that time, that is, the fires were allowed to go out at night thus permitting a cooler and moister atmosphere. It has been found, however, that these are now quite difficult subjects to flower owing to the effect of equal day and night temperatures and to the drying atmosphere produced by central heating, but this ought to be easy to cure by setting the thermostatic control for as low a night temperature as necessary.

In north Germany, too, indoor orchid cultivation has been a hobby for over seventy years, and there are now some truly magnificent 'room gardens' with orchid plants grown to perfection. A very great deal of ingenuity has been exercised both in the construction of these domestic 'greenhouses' and in their lighting and ventilation.

As a result of this long experience, it has been discovered that mixed lighting is best: tungsten and fluorescent together in the proportion of one tungsten to about nine fluorescent tubes. One without the other has been found to boost either flower growth or vegetative growth to the detriment of the whole plant.

In addition to the window-sill method of indoor growing there are various contrivances which are free-standing. The Wardian case, for example, is a cabinet containing lighting at the top, heating at the base, and humidity and growing stages similar to the window 'house'. The sides and top are of glass or plastic, and the whole case is simple to construct. It can be made to whatever proportions are most suitable. For instance, a convenient size for a case to be placed along a wall would be three feet high, five feet long and three feet wide. Another type of construction is a frame with a canopy holding two or more fluorescent tubes underneath which the plants are placed on a metal tray. This is smaller than a Wardian case and could be placed in a small window or narrow alcove.

In addition to the window-sill house, the Wardian case or the small mobile 'planter', a watering can, a syringe, a thermometer and a hygrometer to measure the humidity are necessary. The watering can is probably the most dangerous item in any beginner's equipment, for it is so easy to over-use. The vast generality of orchids, especially the epiphytes, need watering only at intervals; the length of time varies with the genus and the atmospheric conditions of the season, and if a can is lying handy it is a temptation to give a 'wee splash' just to refresh the plants. This urge must be sternly resisted. A syringe giving a fine spray should be used only on the foliage and the top of the compost. The amount of moisture in the air is measured by the hygrometer, and this instrument, used in conjunction with a thermometer, is a good guide to the need for a freshening of the foliage. The optimum humidity varies with the temperature, the warmer the temperature the higher the humidity and vice versa. This is why watering should never be attempted when the temperature is lower than it should be; a range of about 60°F (16°C) up to 90°F (32°C) is roughly what is required.

The type of orchid best suited to indoor orchid growing depends, of course, on what kind of equipment is available. Generally speaking the cool-house Mexican species and primary hybrids are likely to do best in living rooms in the temperate zones of the world, whereas intermediate or even hot-house kinds are easiest in warmer climates and the cool-house the most difficult. In these warmer parts of the world the orchids are brought into the living room from outside only for protection against the weather or for display on special occasions.

The following is a brief list of orchids which are easy to cultivate in living room conditions, provided the essential warmth with a lower night temperature, humidity, ventilation and light are given correctly.

Paphiopedilum species and hybrids do well because they are not too tall and do not require so much light as other genera.

Some of the oncidiums grow too tall for Wardian case or enclosed window-sill cultivation, as do hybrid cymbidiums. Miniature cymbidiums and the smaller oncidiums, however, are ideal.

Miltonias are suitable because they are of a reasonable size and

Coelogyne cristata, a very popular cool-house species. Although a little shy of flowering when young, a large plant has many flowers and will stand some ill treatment.

PL. 501

produce such large, flat blooms relative to the size of the plant. They are also delightfully scented.

Coelogyne cristata is a good plant as it dislikes being repotted and is therefore less bother.

Odontoglossum grande, O. brevifolium, O. bictoniense, O. hallii, O. insleayi and the small-growing hybrids, bi-generic and otherwise, can all be grown successfully.

The lycastes generally, particularly the fragrant *Lycaste aromatica* and *L. deppei,* are good subjects.

Laelia gouldiana and *L. anceps,* will grow well if there is sufficient height.

The *Phalaenopsis* hybrids are a good choice if there is sufficient headroom, and if not, some of the species, such as *P. equestris* and *P. luedemanniana.*

In addition to being suitable for indoor growing the above plants are all readily obtainable, which is an important factor. There are, of course, a great many more, but those listed are a varied selection and are mostly showy and occasionally fragrant specimens.

Perhaps the greatest delight in growing this family of plants, quite apart from the deep satisfaction and excitement when flowering time comes round, is the interest shown by fellow enthusiasts, united by the common bond of love of orchids. Whether they are people with large glasshouses or those with only a plant or two, the bond exists, and the remarkable fact is that there can be few cities in the world where there is not an orchid-grower. Lasting friendships between orchid fanciers of different nationalities have been formed in hundreds and probably thousands. It was once said of a certain Englishman 'He can't be *all* bad, . . . he plays cricket', a debatable statement, which must be truer of an orchid grower. May they proliferate, may they propagate their species, and may they flourish exceedingly.

Index

Page numbers in italic refer to illustrations

Acknowledgements

Photographs are reproduced by courtesy of the following: Trustees of the British Museum 12; The Royal Horticultural Society 19 top, 19 bottom, 20, 70–71, 108.
The pictures used on the titlepage and at the top of page 98 are photographed from paintings by Leslie Greenwood for *Flowers of the World* by Frances Perry, Hamlyn, 1972.
Sources of photographs:

COLOUR
Mike Andrews 58; Armstrong and Brown Nurseries 121 top; Peter Black 76 bottom, 77 top, 77 bottom, 117 top, 124; Anne Bolt 10 top; J. Allan Cash 10 bottom, 35 top, 62, 63 bottom, 65, 113; Bruce Coleman Ltd.– R. Campbell 35 bottom, 102 bottom, 103 top, Bruce Coleman Ltd.–B. J. Coates 7 top, Bruce Coleman Ltd.–N. Myers 7 bottom, 99 top, Bruce Coleman Ltd.–C. Ott 11 top left; Ernest L. Crowson 76 top; Dell Park Nurseries 98 bottom; G. C. K. Dunsterville front jacket, 34 bottom, 39 bottom, 54, 59 top, 63 top, 103 bottom; Hamlyn Group Picture Library titlepage, 14, 15, 38, 50, 68–69, 72, 73, 98 top, back jacket; Peter F. Hunt 68; Natural History Photographic Agency 11 top right, 42, 55, 110; Picturepoint Ltd. 46; Popperfoto 11 bottom, 34 top; David Sander 59 bottom; Harry Smith 39 top, 43 top, 43 bottom, 47, 80, 99 bottom, 102 top, 106–107, 117 bottom, 120, 121 bottom, 125.

BLACK AND WHITE
Peter Black 36 top, 53, 83, 93, 96–97; Camera Press 24–25, 87; J. Allan Cash 26, 28, 32, 49, 115; Bruce Coleman Ltd.–A. E. McR. Pearce 29 right; Ernest L. Crowson 40; Hamlyn Group Picture Library 12, 13, 19 top, 19 bottom, 20, 27, 31, 33, 36 bottom, 45, 57 top, 57 bottom, 66, 67, 70–71, 85, 108, 119, 123; Mansell Collection 9, 29 left, 30; Popperfoto 100–101, 104; Radio Times Hulton Picture Library 60–61, 79, 90, 94; David Sander 16, 16–17, 22–23, 75, 88.